101 Things To Do With

A Dutch Oven

101 Things To Do With A Dutch Oven

BY
VERNON WINTERTON

Gibbs Smith, Publisher
Salt Lake City

First Edition
19 18 17 16 15   30 29 28 27 26 25 24 23 22 21

Published by
Gibbs Smith, Publisher
P.O. Box 667
Layton, Utah 84041

Orders: 1.800.748.5439
www.gibbs-smith.com

Consulting editor: Stephanie Ashcraft
Designed by Kurt Wahlner
Printed and bound in Korea

Library of Congress Cataloging-in-Publication Data

Winterton, Vernon.
101 things to do with a dutch oven / by Vernon Winterton.—1st ed.
p. cm.
ISBN-13: 978-1-58685-785-1
ISBN-10: 1-58685-785-1
1. Dutch oven cookery. I. Title: One hundred one things to do with a dutch oven. II.
Title.

TX840.D88W56 2006
641.5'89—dc22

                              2005020808

This book is dedicated to
my mentor, the man who
taught me to cook in a Dutch
oven, A. Tom Price. Also, to all
my friends who I have cooked
with and learned from. And
especially my wife, Barbara,
whose name should follow
mine in the byline—she helped
me with every recipe.

CONTENTS

Sauces, Soups, & Stews

Fresh Tomato Sauce 80 • Creamy White Mushroom Sauce 81 • Creamy Parmesan Sauce 82 • Good Ol' Dutch Oven Chili 83 • White Chili 84 • Dutch Oven Stew 85 • Kvetcher Stew 86 • Lamb Stew 87 • Tortilla Soup 88 • Chunky Chicken Soup 89 • Hamburger Soup 90

Desserts

Raspberry-Peach Pie 92 • Cherry Pie 93 • Pecan Pie 94 • Lemon Heads Pie 95 • Pear-Raspberry Pie 96 • Chocolate Cake 97 • Banana Cake 98 • Berry-Peach Cobbler 99 • Dump Cobbler 100 • Southern-Style Peach Cobbler 101 • Apple Spice Cake 102 • Chocolate Peppermint Cake 103 • Devil's Food Cake 104 • Lemon-Orange Cake 105 • Pumpkin Crumble 106 • Smacos 107 • Sweet Poached Pears 108 • S'mores Brownies 109 • White Chocolate–Caramel Pecan Cheesecake 110 • Carrot Cake 111 • Apple Cinnamon Cake 112 • Zucchini-Carrot Cake 113 • Pumpkin Spice Cake 114 • Strawberry Torte 115 • Apple Crunch 116 • Oatmeal Cobbler 117 • Snack Cake 118 • Caramel Apple Cobbler 119 • Peachy Dump Cake 120

HELPFUL HINTS

I. Use your Dutch oven year-round—just put it anywhere it will be protected from wind, such as a patio, garage, or even the oven. Wind carries the heat away, so it is important to be in a wind-free area.

2. Charcoal briquettes are used in all recipes of this book. If cooking in your home oven, simply place Dutch oven inside without the coals and set your oven temperature as listed in the recipe.

3. When purchasing a Dutch oven, look for lumps in the casting. Lumps cause hot spots you want to avoid. Look at the thickness of all sides of a Dutch oven. If one side is thinner than the other, it will not cook evenly and your results will be poor. Also, make sure the lid sits flat and does not rock to ensure there is a good seal when cooking. However, if the lid moves side to side slightly, that is fine.

4. All Dutch ovens come with a wax on them to protect during shipping (unless it has been preseasoned). To season a new Dutch oven, scrub off all the wax and then coat with shortening. Place Dutch oven upside down in a barbecue or an oven (to allow shortening to drip off when heating), and heat to 400 degrees for 30 minutes. This begins to make the nonstick surface for which Dutch ovens are famous. Let the oven cool naturally, and when you can touch it with your hands, place the lid back on the Dutch oven and let it continue to cool. The more you use the oven, the more seasoned or nonstick it will become. Depending on the frequency of use, you may have to season several times a year. When the oven starts to smell rancid, do the whole seasoning process again.

5. When you clean a Dutch oven after it has been seasoned, don't use soap. The soap pulls the seasoning out and you will have to season it again. Use really hot water and a plastic scrubbing pad. Never use anything metal. Metal will scrape away the oven's nonstick surface.

6. Store a Dutch oven with something between the lid and the pot, such as a rolled-up paper towel. This allows air to flow through it during

storage and helps keep the oven from becoming rancid. If the oven gives off a funny pungent smell, you know it is rancid and needs to be seasoned again. If you use your oven year-round, it will not become rancid. If your oven becomes rusty, you are not using it often enough. Scrub the rust off with an SOS pad, dry, and then season it again.

7. Heat control is important in a Dutch oven. Take the size of the oven, such as 12-inch, then double that number to 24. This gives you the number of coals to start with to reach 350 degrees of heat. A 14-inch would be 28, a 16-inch would be 32, and so on. Place 10 coals under the Dutch oven and put the rest on top. Each additional coal placed on the oven adds approximately 20 degrees. For baking, put most of the heat on the lid. For frying, put most of the heat on the bottom. You will almost never put a coal in the center of the oven (bottom or lid) as it will make a hot spot and burn food, causing poor results.

8. Experiment with your Dutch oven and get creative with your recipes. You may even want to enter a Dutch oven cook-off. Look at the International Dutch Oven Society Web page for a cook-off near you.

9. When cooking with a Dutch oven, be mindful of the size of your coals so your heat doesn't drop. When coals are the size of a quarter, it's time to replace them with new ones.

10. Rotate Dutch oven every 10 minutes by moving lid counterclockwise and bottom clockwise. This will help to cook more evenly, especially with cakes and breads.

11. Place moisture managers between the lid and the Dutch oven or use clothespins to help hold the lid ajar. This allows the moisture to escape as needed when reducing sauces or liquids in a recipe.

12. The Camp Chef Ultimate Dutch oven is a special Dutch oven that is designed for convection cooking. It has two racks, one on the bottom for cooking the meat, and one near the top for cooking vegetables, and many other uses, such as for cooking pies. They come in either aluminum or cast iron.

BREAKFAST

CINNAMON ROLLS

Dutch oven size: 14-inch

1/2 cup	**sugar**
3/4 cup	**warm water**
2 tablespoons	**active dry yeast**
1 cup	**milk**
1/2 cup	**potato flakes**
3/4 cup	**butter** or **margarine,** softened and divided
1 teaspoon	**salt**
2	**eggs**
4 to 4 1/2 cups	**flour,** divided
3 teaspoons	**cinnamon**
1 1/2 cups	**brown sugar**
1 1/2 cups	**raisins** (optional)
3/4 cup	**chopped pecans** (optional)
1 container	**vanilla** or **cream cheese frosting**

In a large bowl, combine sugar, water, yeast, and milk and then let sit 5 minutes. Add potato flakes and mix well. Mix in 1/2 cup butter, salt, eggs, and 2 cups flour; beat well. Add remaining flour to form a soft, elastic dough. Cover and let rise until double in size. Punch down dough and roll out to 9 x 11 inches, and about 1/4 inch thick. Spread with remaining butter and sprinkle with cinnamon, sugar, and raisins and pecans, if desired. Roll, starting with the longer side, like a jelly roll. Cut 10 to 12 individual rolls using thread or string. Place in Dutch oven sprayed with nonstick spray. Cover and let rise until double in size. Bake at 350 degrees using 12 coals on bottom and 16 on top. Bake 25–30 minutes, or until done. Frost rolls while warm. Makes 10–12 cinnamon rolls.

STICKY BUNS

Dutch oven size: 12-inch

1 cup	**hot milk**
1 tablespoon	**butter** or **margarine**
$1/4$ cup	**warm water**
1 tablespoon	**sugar**
1 tablespoon	**active dry yeast**
$3^1/2$ cups	**flour,** divided
$1/4$ teaspoon	**salt**
1	**egg,** beaten
$1/2$ cup	**butter** or **margarine,** melted
1 cup	**brown sugar**
1 bag (10 ounces)	**pecan gems**

In a small bowl, combine hot milk and butter until butter melts.

In a large bowl, combine water, sugar, and yeast and set aside. In a separate bowl, combine half the flour, salt, egg, and milk-butter mixture. Beat 5 minutes. Add yeast mixture. Add remaining flour and knead on a floured surface 10 minutes or until dough is elastic. Place in Dutch oven sprayed with nonstick spray. Cover with lid and place 3 coals on top to speed up the rising process. Let rise 30 minutes, or until double in size. Remove from Dutch oven and roll into a long log, about 2 to 3 inches in diameter, using your hands. Cut the log into 16 equal pieces. Form a ball with each piece and dip into remaining melted butter about halfway.

Coat buttered side of balls in brown sugar and then roll in pecans. Sprinkle any remaining sugar and pecans in bottom of Dutch oven. Place dough balls, sugar side down, in Dutch oven. Bake 35–40 minutes, or until golden brown, at 350 degrees using 10 coals on bottom and 14 on top. When done, invert sticky buns on plate. Scrape any remaining sauce from Dutch oven and drizzle over top. Makes 16 servings.

APPLE DUMPLING ROLLS

Dutch oven size: 12-inch, 5-inch

2 cups	**flour**
1 teaspoon	**salt**
2 teaspoons	**baking powder**
$^3/_4$ cup	**shortening**
$^1/_2$ cup	**milk**
3 to 4	**apples,** grated
	cinnamon
2 cups	**water**
1 cup	**sugar**
1 cup	**brown sugar**
$^1/_4$ cup	**butter** or **margarine,** melted
$^1/_4$ teaspoon	**cinnamon**

In a bowl, combine flour, salt, and baking powder, and then cut in shortening. Add milk and mix until a soft dough forms. Roll out to 12 x 16 inches, and about $^1/_4$ inch thick. Place grated apples evenly over top and sprinkle with cinnamon. Roll, starting with the longer side, like a jelly roll and cut into 12 rolls using thread or string. Place in 12-inch Dutch oven sprayed with nonstick spray.

In 5-inch Dutch oven, heat water, sugars, butter, and cinnamon until melted together and smooth. Pour over and around rolls. Bake 30 minutes at 350 degrees using 8–10 coals on bottom and 16 on top. Serve warm. Makes 12 rolls.

ORANGE CRANBERRY ROLLS

Dutch oven size: 12-inch

4 teaspoons	**active dry yeast**
2 cups	**warm water,** divided
7 tablespoons	**sugar,** divided
6 cups	**flour**
4 tablespoons	**instant nonfat dry milk**
2 teaspoons	**salt**
6 tablespoons	**butter** or **margarine**
I cup	**dried** or **frozen cranberries**
2 teaspoons	**orange extract**
2	**oranges,** zested

In a bowl, combine yeast, I cup water, 4 tablespoons sugar, and set aside.

In a separate bowl, combine remaining ingredients except remaining water, orange extract, and orange zest. Stir in yeast mixture, orange extract, and orange zest. Add remaining water and knead dough until elastic. Place in greased bowl and turn to coat. Cover and let rise 30 minutes, or until double in size. Punch down dough and form into 16 balls. Place in warm Dutch oven sprayed with nonstick spray. Cover and let rise until double in size. Bake 20–30 minutes, or until done, at 350 degrees using 10 coals on bottom and 14 on top. Makes 16 rolls.

RAISIN BREAD

Dutch oven size: 10-inch

1 1/2 cups plus 1 tablespoon	**warm water**
4 tablespoons	**sugar**
1 tablespoon	**active dry yeast**
3 3/4 cups	**flour**
3 tablespoons	**instant nonfat dry milk**
2 1/4 teaspoons	**salt**
1 tablespoon	**cinnamon**
3 tablespoons	**butter** or **margarine,** softened
1 1/2 cups	**raisins**
1/2 cup	**chopped nuts** (optional)

In a bowl, combine water, sugar, and yeast and set aside.

In a separate bowl, mix flour, dry milk, salt, cinnamon, butter, raisins, and nuts, if desired. Add yeast mixture and knead until a soft dough forms. Place in greased bowl and turn to coat. Cover and let rise 45 minutes, or until double in size. Punch down dough, form a loaf, and place in warm Dutch oven sprayed with nonstick spray. Cover and let rise until double in size. Bake 40 minutes, or until golden brown, at 350 degrees using 8 coals on bottom and 12 on top. Makes 12 servings.

BREAKFAST ROLLS

Dutch oven size: 12-inch

	oil
1 heaping cup	**cooked, crumbled bacon pieces**
$^3/_4$ cup	**chopped mushrooms**
3 tablespoons	**chopped red onion**
9 ounces	**evaporated milk**
6 tablespoons	**butter** or **margarine**
$^1/_2$ cup	**water**
$4^1/_2$ cups	**flour**
$5^1/_4$ tablespoons	**sugar**
$1^1/_2$ teaspoons	**salt**
3 teaspoons	**yeast**
$^3/_4$ cup	**grated medium cheddar cheese**

Drizzle small amount of oil in bottom of Dutch oven. Place bacon, mushrooms, and onion in oil and cook until mushrooms are tender. Remove mixture from Dutch oven and set aside, leaving oils in Dutch oven. Add milk and butter to the oven and heat until butter is melted. Pour into bowl and add water. Add remaining ingredients and mix well, kneading 2–5 minutes. Place dough in greased bowl and turn to coat. Cover and let rise until double in size. Punch down dough and divide into 16 balls. Place in Dutch oven sprayed with nonstick spray. Cover and let rise until double in size. Bake 30–40 minutes at 375 degrees using 9 coals on bottom and 15 on top. Makes 16 rolls.

CINNAMON PULL-A-PARTS

Dutch oven size: 12-inch

2 cups	**warm water**
1/3 cup	**sugar**
2 tablespoons	**active dry yeast**
1/3 cup	**oil**
1 1/2 teaspoons	**salt**
1	**egg**
2/3 cup	**instant nonfat dry milk**
5 to 6 cups	**flour,** divided
1/2 cup	**butter** or **margarine,** melted
1 tablespoon	**cinnamon,** or to taste
1 1/2 cups	**brown sugar**

In a large bowl, combine water, sugar, and yeast and set aside 5 minutes. Add oil, salt, and egg. Combine dry milk with 2 cups flour and add to yeast mixture. Beat until smooth. Add remaining flour, 1 cup at a time, and mix until smooth. Knead dough until elastic, and then place in greased bowl and turn to coat. Cover and let rise until triple in size.

Form into 16 balls and then dip in melted butter. In a small bowl, combine cinnamon and sugar. Roll balls in cinnamon mixture and then place in warm Dutch oven sprayed with nonstick spray. Pour any leftover cinnamon and sugar mixture over top. Bake 15–20 minutes at 350 degrees using 10 coals on bottom and 14 on top. When done, loosen edges with knife and move rolls to wire rack to cool. Makes 16 servings.

ROYAL BRAID

Dutch oven size: 12-inch

2 cups	**warm water**
1 cup plus 3 tablespoons	**sugar**
2 tablespoons plus $^1/_2$ teaspoon	**active dry yeast**
3 teaspoons	**salt**
3 tablespoons	**butter** or **margarine**
1 cup plus 1 to 2 tablespoons	**milk,** divided
7$^1/_2$ cups	**flour,** divided
$^1/_2$ cup	**butter** or **margarine,** melted and divided
$^1/_2$ cup	**brown sugar**
1 tablespoon	**cinnamon**
1 cup	**powdered sugar**
$^1/_2$ teaspoon	**vanilla**
$^1/_2$ cup	**chopped pecans**

In a bowl, combine water, $^2/_3$ cup sugar, and yeast. When foamy, add salt, 3 tablespoons butter, 1 cup milk, and 5 cups flour. Stir until mixed, then add remaining flour $^1/_2$ cup at a time. Knead until a soft dough forms. Cover and let rise 45 minutes, or until double in size. Punch down dough and roll out into large rectangle. Brush with half the melted butter.

In a small bowl, combine remaining sugar, brown sugar, and cinnamon and then sprinkle over top. Fold rectangle into thirds then roll out to a rectangle again. Divide rectangle lengthwise into 3 equal pieces and braid together. Bring ends in to form a wreath and then place in Dutch oven sprayed with nonstick spray. Bake 45–55 minutes at 350 degrees using 10 coals on bottom and 14 on top. When golden brown, remove from oven and brush with remaining butter and let cool.

In a bowl, mix together powdered sugar, remaining milk, and vanilla. Drizzle over cooled braid and then sprinkle with nuts. Makes 16 servings.

MOUNTAIN MAN BREAKFAST

Dutch oven size: 12-inch

1 pound	**bacon**
1 pound	**sausage**
2 packages (24 ounces each)	**frozen southern-style hash browns** (not shredded)
1 container (8 ounces)	**sour cream**
4	**eggs,** beaten
1 pound	**grated sharp cheddar cheese**

Brown bacon and sausage in Dutch oven. Stir in hash browns and cover. Bake 25–30 minutes at 350 degrees using 10 coals on bottom and 14 on top.

In a bowl, combine sour cream and eggs. Pour over hash browns about 5 minutes before they are done. Cover and let cook 5 minutes, or until eggs are cooked through. When done, remove lid and sprinkle cheese over top. Replace lid until cheese melts. Makes 20 servings.

BREAKFAST PIZZA

Dutch oven size: 14-inch

1 pound	**sausage**
1	**green bell pepper,** chopped
1	**medium onion,** chopped
1 package (8 ounces)	**sliced mushrooms**
3 tubes (8 ounces each)	**refrigerator biscuits**
10	**eggs,** well beaten
1	**medium tomato,** chopped
1 can (4 ounces)	**sliced olives**
$^1/_2$ pound	**grated Monterey Jack cheese**
$^1/_2$ pound	**grated mozzarella cheese**

Cook sausage with bell pepper, onion, and mushrooms in Dutch oven. Drain excess grease and remove. In same Dutch oven, arrange biscuits on bottom, and then spoon sausage mixture over top. Pour eggs over sausage mixture. Sprinkle tomato, olives, and cheeses over top. Bake 30 minutes at 325 degrees using 8 coals on bottom and 16 on top. Serve with salsa on the side. Makes 8 servings.

BREAKFAST CASSEROLE

Dutch oven size: 12-inch

1 package (24 ounces)	**frozen shredded potatoes**
$^1/_3$ cup	**butter** or **margarine,** melted
1 cup	**grated cheddar cheese**
1 cup	**grated Swiss cheese**
1 cup	**cooked and cubed ham**
6	**eggs**
$^1/_2$ cup	**milk**
$^1/_2$ teaspoon	**salt**

Brown potatoes in butter in a warm Dutch oven and then spread evenly over bottom. Sprinkle cheese and ham over top.

In a separate bowl, beat eggs, milk, and salt together. Pour over ham and cheese. Bake 30–35 minutes at 350 degrees using 10 coals on bottom and 14 on top. Makes 8 servings.

BREADS & ROLLS

POTATO BREAD

Dutch oven size: 10-inch

1 cup plus 2 tablespoons	**warm water**
1 1/2 tablespoons	**sugar**
2 teaspoons	**active dry yeast**
3 cups	**flour**
1/2 cup	**instant potato flakes**
1 1/2 tablespoons	**nonfat instant dry milk**
1 1/2 teaspoons	**salt**
1 1/2 tablespoons	**butter** or **margarine,** softened

In a bowl, combine water, sugar, and yeast and set aside.

In a separate bowl, mix flour, potato flakes, dry milk, salt, and butter. Add yeast mixture and knead until a soft dough forms. Place in greased bowl and turn to coat. Cover and let rise until double in size. Punch down dough and form a loaf. Place in warm Dutch oven sprayed with nonstick spray. Cover and let rise until double in size. Bake 40 minutes, or until golden brown, at 350 degrees using 8 coals on bottom and 12 on top. Makes 12 servings.

GARLIC BREAD

Dutch oven size: 10-inch

1 cup plus 2 tablespoons	**warm water**
1 tablespoon	**sugar**
2 teaspoons	**active dry yeast**
3 cups	**flour**
1 tablespoon	**instant nonfat dry milk**
1 1/2 teaspoons	**salt**
1 tablespoon	**dried parsley flakes**
1 1/2 to 3 teaspoons	**garlic powder,** or to taste
1 tablespoon	**butter** or **margarine,** softened

In a bowl, combine water, sugar, and yeast and set aside.

In a separate bowl, mix flour, dry milk, salt, parsley, and garlic powder. Add the yeast mixture and butter and then knead until a soft dough forms. Place in greased bowl and turn to coat. Cover and let rise until double in size. Punch down dough, form a loaf, and then place in warm Dutch oven sprayed with nonstick spray. Cover and let rise until double in size. Bake 40 minutes, or until golden brown, at 350 degrees using 8 coals on bottom and 12 on top. Makes 12 servings.

DRIED ONION BREAD

Dutch oven size: 12-inch

2 cups plus 1 tablespoon	**buttermilk***
3 tablespoons	**butter** or **margarine,** softened
3 tablespoons	**molasses**
1 envelope	**onion soup mix**
3³/₄ cups	**flour**
³/₄ cup	**cornmeal**
3 teaspoons	**active dry yeast**

In a bowl, combine buttermilk, butter, and molasses. Add soup mix, flour, and cornmeal. Add yeast and then knead until a soft dough forms. Cover and let rise until double in size. Punch down dough and form a loaf. Place in warm Dutch oven sprayed with nonstick spray. Cover and let rise until double in size. Bake 40 minutes, or until golden brown, at 350 degrees using 10 coals on bottom and 14 on top. Makes 12 servings.

*You may make your own buttermilk by combining 1³/₄ cups milk with ¹/₄ cup lemon juice.

BASIC WHITE BREAD

Dutch oven size: 12-inch

1 cup	**warm water**
2 tablespoons	**sugar**
2 teaspoons	**active dry yeast**
2³/₄ cups	**flour**
2 tablespoons	**instant nonfat dry milk**
1³/₄ teaspoons	**salt**
2 tablespoons	**butter** or **margarine,** softened

In a bowl, combine water, sugar, and yeast and set aside.

In a separate bowl, mix flour, dry milk, and salt. Add butter and yeast mixture. Knead until a soft dough forms. Place in greased bowl and turn to coat. Cover and let rise until double in size. Punch down dough and form a loaf. Place in warm Dutch oven sprayed with nonstick spray. Cover and let rise until double in size. Bake at 350 degrees for 40 minutes, or until golden brown, using 10 coals on bottom and 14 on top. Makes 12 servings.

ITALIAN HERB BREAD

Dutch oven size: 10-inch

1 cup plus 1 tablespoon	**warm water**
1 tablespoon	**sugar**
1 1/2 teaspoons	**active dry yeast**
2 3/4 cups	**flour**
1 tablespoon	**instant nonfat dry milk**
1 1/2 teaspoons	**salt**
1/4 cup	**grated fresh Parmesan** or **asiago cheese**
2 teaspoons	**Italian seasoning**
2 tablespoons	**butter** or **margarine,** softened

In a bowl, combine water, sugar, and yeast and set aside.

In a separate bowl, mix flour, dry milk, salt, cheese, and Italian seasoning. Add butter and yeast mixture and knead until a soft dough forms. Place in greased bowl and turn to coat. Cover and let rise until double in size. Punch down dough, form a loaf, and place in warm Dutch oven sprayed with nonstick spray. Cover and let rise until double in size. Bake 40 minutes, or until golden brown, at 350 degrees using 8 coals on bottom and 12 on top. Makes 12 servings.

RUSSIAN BLACK BREAD

Dutch oven size: 12-inch

2 1/2 cups	**flour**
1 cup	**rye flour**
1 teaspoon	**salt**
2 tablespoons	**brown sugar**
3 tablespoons	**unsweetened cocoa powder**
1 tablespoon	**caraway seeds**
1/4 teaspoon	**fennel seeds**
2 teaspoons	**active dry yeast**
4 teaspoons	**Postum***
2 tablespoons	**vinegar**
2 tablespoons	**butter** or **margarine,** softened
2 tablespoons	**dark corn syrup**
1 1/2 cups	**hot water**

In a bowl, combine all dry ingredients. Add remaining ingredients and knead until a soft dough forms. Place in greased bowl and turn to coat. Cover and let rise 30 minutes, or until double in size. Punch down dough and knead again. Form a loaf and place in Dutch oven sprayed with nonstick spray. Cover and let rise until double in size. Bake 30–40 minutes at 350 degrees using 10 coals on bottom and 14 on top. Makes 16 servings.

* 1 teaspoon instant coffee granules may be substituted.

SIMPLE FRENCH BREAD

Dutch oven size: 12-inch

3 cups	**warm water**
2 tablespoons	**sugar**
2 tablespoons	**active dry yeast**
I tablespoon	**salt**
8 cups	**flour,** divided

In a large bowl, combine water, sugar, yeast, and salt and set aside 5 minutes. Add 4 cups flour and mix well. Gradually add remaining flour and mix until a soft dough forms and then knead until elastic. Cover and let rise 10 minutes, then knead 8 minutes. (The longer you knead, the tougher the crust will be, thus creating a true French bread.) Form a loaf and place in warm Dutch oven sprayed with nonstick spray. Cover and let rise until double in size. Bake 30 minutes at 350 degrees using 10 coals on bottom and 14 on top. Makes 12 servings.

JALAPENO CHEESE BREAD

Dutch oven size: 12-inch

3 tablespoons	**butter** or **margarine,** divided
3	**eggs,** separated into yolks and whites
3 tablespoons	**sugar**
2 cups	**milk**
$^2/_3$ cup	**cornmeal**
$^2/_3$ cup	**flour**
I teaspoon	**salt**
2 teaspoons	**baking powder**
I pinch	**salt**
$^1/_3$ cup	**grated jalapeno pepper jack cheese**

Preheat Dutch oven using 10 coals on bottom and 14 on top. Melt I tablespoon butter in bottom.

In a bowl, combine remaining butter, egg yolks, and sugar. Mix well, then add milk, cornmeal, flour, I teaspoon salt, and baking powder.

In a separate bowl, whip egg whites and a pinch of salt until soft peaks form. Fold into flour mixture, along with cheese. Bake 20–25 minutes at 350 degrees using 10 coals on bottom and 14 on top. Sprinkle more cheese over top during last 5 minutes of baking and let melt. Makes 16 servings.

SOURDOUGH BREAD

Dutch oven size: 14-inch

3 cups	**hot water**
2 tablespoons	**sugar**
2 tablespoons	**active dry yeast**
1 tablespoon	**salt**
2 cups	**Sourdough Starter** (see Breads & Rolls, page 41)
9 cups	**flour**

In a large bowl, combine water, sugar, and yeast and set aside 5 minutes. Stir in salt and Sourdough Starter. Add 4 cups flour and stir until dough is smooth. Gradually add enough remaining flour to make dough workable and not sticky. Knead until smooth and elastic. Place in greased bowl and turn to coat. Cover and let rise 60 minutes, or until double in size. Punch down dough every 10 minutes. Remove from bowl and separate into two loaves. Cover and let rise 10 minutes. Place in warm Dutch oven sprayed with nonstick spray. Cover and let rise until double in size. Bake 30–40 minutes at 375 degrees using 10 coals on bottom and 16 on top. Makes 24 servings.

BASIC DINNER ROLLS

Dutch oven size: 12-inch

2$^{1}/_{2}$ cups	**warm water**
5 tablespoons	**sugar**
2 tablespoons	**active dry yeast**
1 tablespoon	**salt**
5 tablespoons	**oil**
7 to 7$^{1}/_{2}$ cups	**flour,** divided

In a bowl, combine water, sugar, and yeast and set aside 5 minutes. Add salt and oil and mix well. Add 4 cups flour and mix until smooth. Gradually add enough remaining flour, about 3 to 3$^{1}/_{2}$ cups, until a soft dough forms. Knead until elastic. Place in greased bowl and turn to coat. Cover and let rise until double in size. Punch down dough and knead again. Form 16 balls and place in warm Dutch oven sprayed with nonstick spray. Cover and let rise until double in size. Bake 30 minutes at 350 degrees using 10 coals on bottom and 14 on top. Immediately remove from Dutch oven to cool. Makes 16 servings.

CRESCENT ROLLS

Dutch oven size: 12-inch

1 1/3 cups	**scalded milk**
2 tablespoons	**butter** or **margarine**
4 tablespoons	**sugar**
1 teaspoon	**salt**
4 1/2 teaspoons	**yeast**
1/4 cup	**warm water**
2	**eggs,** well beaten
4 1/2 cups	**flour**

In a bowl, combine milk, butter, sugar, and salt. Let cool to room temperature.

In a separate bowl, combine yeast and water, and then add cooled milk mixture and eggs. Add 2 1/2 cups flour and mix until well blended. Gradually add remaining flour until a soft dough forms. Place in greased bowl and turn to coat. Cover and let rise until double in size. Punch down dough and divide into 2 equal parts. Roll each out to a 12-inch circle on a floured surface. Cut each circle into 8 triangles and roll up, starting with the wide end and finishing with the point, then bend ends in slightly to form a crescent shape. Place in Dutch oven sprayed with nonstick spray. Bake 20–25 minutes, or until golden brown, at 350 degrees using 10 coals on bottom and 14 on top. Makes 16 rolls.

ROLLS SUPREME

Dutch oven size: 12-inch

1 1/4 cups	**warm water,** divided
1/4 cup	**sugar**
1 tablespoon	**active dry yeast**
1/2 teaspoon	**salt**
1 tablespoon	**Salad Supreme seasoning**
1/2 cup	**butter** or **margarine,** melted
2	**eggs**
3 to 5 cups	**flour**
1	**egg white,** slightly whipped

In a bowl, combine 1/4 cup water, sugar, and yeast and set aside.

In a separate bowl, mix remaining water, salt, Salad Supreme, butter, and 2 eggs. Stir in 1 cup flour until well blended. Add yeast mixture. Gradually add remaining flour and knead until smooth. Cover and let rise 45 minutes, or until double in size. Punch down dough and form 16 balls. Place in Dutch oven sprayed with nonstick spray. Cover and let rise until double in size. Brush with egg white, then sprinkle with more Salad Supreme. Bake 25 minutes, or until golden brown, at 425 degrees using 10 coals on bottom and 19 on top. Makes 16 rolls.

ONE-BOWL DINNER ROLLS

Dutch oven size: 12-inch

2³/₄ to 3¹/₄ cups	**flour,** divided
³/₄ cup	**sugar**
¹/₂ teaspoon	**salt**
2 tablespoons	**active dry yeast**
5¹/₃ tablespoons	**soft margarine**
²/₃ cup	**hot water**
I	**egg,** beaten and at room temperature
I teaspoon	**garlic powder**
I teaspoon	**onion powder**
2 teaspoons	**rosemary**

In a large bowl, mix ³/₄ cup flour, sugar, salt, and yeast. Add soft margarine and water. Stir until a thick batter forms. Stir in egg, ¹/₂ cup flour, garlic powder, onion powder, and rosemary. Knead in bowl, gradually adding enough remaining flour until a soft dough forms. Knead 2 minutes or until smooth. Place back in bowl. Cover and let rise until double in size. Punch down dough, form 16 balls, and place in warm Dutch oven sprayed with nonstick spray. Cover and let rise until double in size. Bake 10–15 minutes, or until golden brown, at 375 degrees using 10 coals on bottom and 16 on top. Makes 16 rolls.

PUMPERNICKEL ROLLS

Dutch oven size: 10-inch

4$\frac{1}{2}$ teaspoons	**active dry yeast**
1 tablespoon	**sugar**
1$\frac{1}{4}$ cups	**warm water**
1 cup	**rye flour**
1 cup	**wheat flour**
$\frac{1}{4}$ cup	**molasses**
2 tablespoons	**cocoa**
1 tablespoon	**caraway seeds**
1$\frac{1}{4}$ teaspoons	**salt**
1$\frac{1}{2}$ cups plus 2 tablespoons	**flour**

In a bowl, combine yeast, sugar, and water and set aside 5 minutes. Add rye and wheat flours, molasses, cocoa, caraway seeds, and salt and mix well. Stir in 1 cup flour then place on floured surface. Knead 5 minutes, adding more flour gradually and only if necessary, until dough is smooth and elastic. Cover and let rise 60 minutes, or until double in size. Punch down dough and form 12 balls, and then place in warm Dutch oven sprayed with nonstick spray. Cover and let rise 30 minutes. Bake 30 minutes at 350 degrees using 8 coals on bottom and 12 on top. Makes 12 rolls.

LICORICE DILL ROLLS

Dutch oven size: 14-inch

7 tablespoons	**sugar,** divided
4 teaspoons	**active dry yeast**
2 cups	**hot water,** divided
6 cups	**flour**
4 tablespoons	**instant nonfat dry milk**
2 teaspoons	**salt**
4 teaspoons	**dill weed**
2 teaspoons	**fennel seeds**
6 tablespoons	**butter** or **margarine,** melted

In a bowl, mix 3 tablespoons sugar, yeast, and 1 cup hot water and set aside.

In a separate bowl, combine remaining dry ingredients. Add yeast mixture, butter, and remaining water. Mix until dough is elastic. Place dough in lightly greased bowl and turn to coat. Cover and let rise 30 minutes, or until double in size. Punch down dough and form into 16 balls. Place in warm Dutch oven sprayed with nonstick spray. Cover and let rise until double in size. Bake at 350 degrees using 10–12 coals on bottom and 16–18 on top. Bake 20–25 minutes, or until done. Makes 16 rolls.

GOLDEN HONEY SOURDOUGH ROLLS

Dutch oven size: 12-inch

2 cups	**scalded milk**
2 tablespoons	**butter** or **margarine**
$^1/_4$ cup	**honey**
1 tablespoon	**active dry yeast**
4 cups	**Sourdough Starter** (see Breads & Rolls, page 41)
2 cups	**wheat flour**
$^1/_4$ cup	**wheat germ** (optional)
2 teaspoons	**baking soda**
2 tablespoons	**salt**
2 tablespoons	**sugar**
2 cups	**flour**

In a bowl, combine milk, butter, and honey and stir until mixed. Cool to lukewarm and then add yeast. Stir until dissolved.

In a separate bowl, combine Sourdough Starter, wheat flour, and wheat germ, if desired.

In a small bowl, combine baking soda, salt, and sugar and then combine gently with sourdough mixture. Add yeast mixture and mix well. Cover and let sit 30 minutes. Stir down dough and gradually add remaining flour until too stiff to stir with a spoon (amount of flour may vary). Place on a floured surface and knead until elastic. Place in greased bowl and turn to coat. Cover and let rise until double in size. Punch down dough and form into 16 balls. Place in warm Dutch oven, cover, and let rise until double in size. Bake 20 minutes at 350 degrees using 10 coals on bottom and 14 on top. Remove from Dutch oven and cool. Makes 16 rolls.

PARMESAN HERB ROLLS

Dutch oven size: 12-inch

I cup	**warm milk**
I cup	**warm water**
4¹/₂ teaspoons	**active dry yeast**
6 tablespoons	**butter** or **margarine,** melted
3	**eggs,** well beaten
I teaspoon	**salt**
¹/₂ cup	**sugar**
I teaspoon	**garlic powder**
I teaspoon	**onion powder**
I teaspoon	**dried rosemary,** crushed
3 tablespoons	**grated Parmesan cheese** (fresh works best)
6¹/₂ cups	**flour**

In a large bowl, combine milk, water, and yeast. Add all remaining ingredients except flour. Add 3 cups flour and mix well. Gradually add remaining flour and knead until a soft dough forms. Place in greased bowl and turn to coat. Cover and let rise until double in size. Punch down dough and form 16 balls. Divide each ball in half and then roll the halves into 6-inch ropes. Braid two ropes together and place in Dutch oven sprayed with nonstick spray. Cover and let rise until double in size. Bake 20–30 minutes, or until golden brown, at 375 degrees using 10 coals on bottom and 16 on top. Remove from Dutch oven and sprinkle with more cheese. Cool on wire rack. Makes 16 rolls.

SOURDOUGH STARTER

2 cups **flour**
2 cups **warm water**
I envelope **active dry yeast**

Combine ingredients in a large bowl (not metal) and mix together until well blended. Let stand in a warm place (80–85 degrees) for 48 hours. Stir well before use. Pour out amount required by recipe and replenish remaining start with the same amount taken out. For example, if 2 cups were taken out, mix in I cup flour and I cup warm water; if three cups were used, mix in I ^{1}/$_2$ cups flour and I ^{1}/$_2$ cups warm water. Let stand in a warm place a few hours until it bubbles. Cover loosely and refrigerate. Use and replenish every few weeks. When measuring flour, spoon into measuring cup and level off. Do not scoop with the cup. Makes 3 cups.

MAIN DISHES

DUTCH OVEN POT ROAST

Dutch oven size: 12-inch

1 envelope	**onion soup mix**
3 to 4 pound	**beef roast**
1 1/2 cups	**water,** divided
2	**beef bouillon cubes**
1/2 pound	**baby carrots**
8 to 10	**medium red** or **new potatoes**
2 tablespoons	**flour**
1/2 cup	**water**

Rub soup mix into roast, then brown roast on all sides in Dutch oven. Add 1 cup water and bouillon. Cover and bake 30 minutes at 350 degrees using 10 coals on bottom and 14 on top. Check and add water as needed, keeping bottom of pan full. Add carrots and potatoes and bake 30 minutes or more. Roast is done when internal temperature reaches 160 degrees. Remove from oven and set aside. Remove vegetables and place in a bowl. Cover to keep warm. Bring liquid in oven to a boil, and then add flour and remaining water, stirring to make gravy. Makes 6–8 servings.

CHICKEN ROLL-UPS

Dutch oven size: 12-inch

> 4 to 6 **thin slices ham**
> 4 to 6 **slices asiago cheese**
> 4 to 6 **boneless, skinless chicken breasts,**
>   flattened to $1/4$ inch thick
> 4 to 6 **slices peppered bacon** (optional)
>   **Creamy White Mushroom Sauce** (see
>   Sauces, Soups, & Stews, page 81)
>   **salt and pepper,** to taste

Place a slice of ham and cheese on each chicken breast, then roll like a jelly roll and secure with a toothpick. Wrap peppered bacon around chicken breast, if desired, before securing with toothpick. Place in Dutch oven containing Creamy White Mushroom Sauce and bake 30–40 minutes at 350 degrees using 10 coals on bottom and 14 on top. Season with salt and pepper. Makes 4–6 servings.

VARIATION: For bacon lovers, use 2 strips bacon per chicken breast.

SAUSAGE SPINACH WREATH

Dutch oven size: 12-inch Camp Chef Ultimate*

¹/₂ pound	**fresh ground pork,** browned and drained
¹/₂ pound	**pork sausage,** browned and drained
1 package (8 ounces)	**cream cheese,** softened
1 small can	**water chestnuts,** drained and chopped
1 box (1.4 ounces)	**Knorr vegetable soup mix**
6 ounces	**chopped frozen spinach,** thawed
1 to 2	**green onions,** chopped (green part only)
2 sheets	**frozen puff pastry,** thawed

In a bowl, mix all ingredients except pastry, cover, and set aside. Cut off corners of both sheets of pastry, making them into large circles. Cut each circle into 8 wedges, for a total of 16.

Cover Dutch oven rack with parchment paper and then arrange 7 wedges in a circle with wide edges touching or slightly overlapping and points facing out. Place 7 more wedges in the circle, laying opposite of the first 7, wide ends slightly overlapping and points facing center; discard unused pastry. You should now have points inside and outside the circle. Place meat mixture in a ring over wide-end seams of wedges. Beginning with last wedge that was placed on the rack, lift point and lay across meat mixture, then lift point of wedge on opposite side and lay across meat mixture. Continue alternating until a wreath is formed. Place rack in warm Dutch oven and bake 40–50 minutes at 400 degrees using 15 coals on bottom and 20 on top. Makes 12–16 servings.

*Tie a string onto the Ultimate rack to help lift wreath out of the oven when done baking.

STUFFED PORK ROAST

Dutch oven size: 14-inch

2- to 3-pound	**boneless pork roast**
	salt and pepper, to taste
2 tablespoons	**toasted pine nuts**
$^1/_2$ cup	**chopped fresh mint**
$^1/_2$ cup	**chopped fresh parsley**
6 to 8	**cloves garlic,** crushed
$^1/_2$ cup	**grated Parmesan cheese**
1	**lemon,** juiced
2 tablespoons	**olive oil,** divided
	Fresh Tomato Sauce (see Sauces, Soups, & Stews, page 80)

Place meat on a cutting board and slice lengthwise down the center of the roast, cutting only two-thirds through. Press each side apart and then slice each side lengthwise down the center, cutting two-thirds through. Pound roast until it lays flat. Add salt and pepper to taste.

In a bowl, combine nuts, mint, parsley, garlic, cheese, lemon juice, and 1 tablespoon oil. Stir together and spread evenly on roast. Roll roast together tightly, filling on the inside, like a jelly roll, and tie together with string to secure. Season with more salt and pepper. Heat Dutch oven using 10 coals on bottom and 16 on top. Add remaining oil and brown rolled roast on all sides. Add Fresh Tomato Sauce to oven and bring to a boil. Reduce heat to a simmer by removing several coals. Cover and simmer gently 60 minutes, turning roast a few times while cooking. When the internal temperature reaches 145 degrees, remove from heat and let sit 15 minutes. Remove string and slice into $^1/_2$-inch pieces. Serve drizzled with warm Fresh Tomato Sauce. Makes 8 servings.

STUFFED PORK IN FRESH TOMATO SAUCE

Dutch oven size: 12-inch

$^2/_3$ small can	**water chestnuts,** drained and chopped
6 to 8 ounces	**frozen chopped spinach,** partially thawed
1 package (8 ounces)	**cream cheese,** softened
1 to 2	**green onions,** chopped (green part only)
1 box (1.4 ounces)	**Knorr vegetable soup mix**
2 (1 pound each)	**pork tenderloins**
	oil
	Fresh Tomato Sauce (see Sauces, Soups, & Stews, page 80)

In a bowl, combine water chestnuts, spinach, cream cheese, green onion, and soup mix and set aside.

With a sharp knife, make a lengthwise cut down the center of each tenderloin, cutting two-thirds through. Press sides apart and make 2 additional lengthwise cuts down the middle of each side, cutting two-thirds through.

In a frying pan, sear tenderloins on all sides in a small amount of oil. Once cool, spread half the filling mixture in each and roll like a jelly roll. Tie with string to secure. Place in Dutch oven and pour Fresh Tomato Sauce over top. Bake 35–40 minutes, or until the internal temperature reaches 160 degrees, at 350 degrees using 10 coals on bottom and 14 on top. Makes 8 servings.

STUFFED CHOPS IN MUSHROOM GRAVY

Dutch oven size: 12-inch

I package (8 ounces)	**sliced mushrooms,** divided
3 cups	**breadcrumbs**
3 to 4	**green onions**
1/3	**red bell pepper**
2	**cloves garlic**
I	**celery stalk**
1/2 teaspoon	**salt**
1 3/4 teaspoons	**ground sage**
1/2 cup	**sunflower seeds**
6 tablespoons	**butter** or **margarine,** melted
1/2 cup	**evaporated milk**
4	**pork chops,** about I inch thick
1/2 cup	**pork seasoning,** divided
I envelope	**onion gravy mix**

Chop half the mushrooms, breadcrumbs, green onions, bell pepper, garlic, and celery, and then mix together with salt, sage, sunflower seeds, butter, and milk, until moist. Set aside in refrigerator. Using a sharp knife, slice two-thirds through pork chops, making a pocket in center. Rub pork chops with 1/4 cup pork seasoning and brown in Dutch oven on both sides. Remove from oven and refrigerate.

Make gravy according to package directions and add remaining pork seasoning, along with remaining mushrooms. Remove pork chops and filling from refrigerator. Stuff pork chops with filling, and then secure with toothpick, if necessary. Place chops back in Dutch oven and pour gravy over top. Bake 30–40 minutes at 350 degrees using 10 coals on bottom and 14 on top. When the internal temperature reaches 165 degrees, remove from Dutch oven and serve. Makes 4 servings.

BEST-EVER BRATWURST

Dutch oven size: 12-inch

4 **bratwurst,** cut into 1-inch slices
1 **head cabbage,** shredded
3 **large carrots,** shredded

Spray Dutch oven with nonstick spray and then cook bratwurst using 14 coals on bottom. Add cabbage and carrots. Cover and add 10 coals on top. Bake 5 minutes, or until vegetables are cooked, but still firm. Makes 6 servings.

TERIYAKI BARBECUE CHICKEN

Dutch oven size: 14-inch

1 bottle (18 ounces)	**barbecue sauce**
1 bottle (18 ounces)	**teriyaki sauce**
6 to 8	**boneless, skinless chicken breasts**
1 can (12 ounces)	**lemon-lime soda**

Pour sauces into Dutch oven and add chicken. Pour soda over top. Bake 30 minutes at 350 degrees using 12 coals on bottom and 16 on top. Chicken is done when internal temperature is 170 degrees, or when pierced with a fork, the juices run clear. Makes 6–8 servings.

DUTCH OVEN PIZZA

Dutch oven size: 12-inch

$^3/_4$ cup	**warm water**
2 tablespoons	**vegetable oil**
2 cups	**flour**
$^1/_2$ teaspoon	**sugar**
$^1/_2$ teaspoon	**salt**
2 teaspoons	**yeast**
	tomato sauce
	pizza toppings
2 cups	**grated mozzarella cheese**

In a bowl, combine water, oil, flour, sugar, salt, and yeast. Cover and let rise 20–30 minutes. Place dough in Dutch oven sprayed with non-stick spray. Flatten gently, pressing from center to the edges of oven and slightly up the sides to form a crust. Spread desired amount of tomato sauce over crust, then layer with pizza toppings, ending with cheese. Bake 20–25 minutes at 425 degrees using 10 coals on bottom and 18 on top. Carefully remove pizza from oven by tilting gently while a helper slides spatulas under the crust and guides it onto a tray. Makes 8 servings.

VARIATION: Need a bigger pizza? Double ingredients and bake in a 14-inch Dutch oven using 12 coals on bottom and 20 on top.

PORK AND STUFFING

Dutch oven size: 12-inch

2¹/₂-pound **pork roast,** cut into 1-inch pieces
2 cans (10.5 ounces each) **cream of mushroom soup,**
condensed
1 package (8 ounces) **sliced mushrooms**
2 boxes (6 ounces each) **stuffing mix**

Brown roast pieces in Dutch oven using 30 coals on bottom only, and
then drain. Add soup and stir. Remove enough coals to reach a simmer
and bake 30–45 minutes to tenderize roast. Layer mushrooms over top.

In a saucepan, make stuffing according to package directions. Spoon
over mushrooms. Bake 30 minutes at 350 degrees using 10 new coals
on bottom and 14 new on top. Makes 12 servings.

CHICKEN PILLOWS

Dutch oven size: 12-inch

> 2 **boneless, skinless chicken breasts,** cut into 1-inch pieces
> 2 **bunches green onions,** sliced (using white part only)
> 1 package (8 ounces) **cream cheese,** softened
> 2 tubes (8 ounces each) **refrigerated crescent roll dough**

Brown and cook chicken pieces thoroughly in Dutch oven and remove to cool. Cut green onions into slices $1/8$ inch thick or less. Stir onions into cream cheese. Add cooled chicken to cream cheese mixture and mix well. Open crescent rolls and separate into individual triangles. Using a tablespoon, place a scoop of chicken mixture in each roll and roll up like a jelly roll, starting with the wide end. There should be enough mixture to fill 16 rolls. Place in Dutch oven and bake 12–15 minutes at 350 degrees using 10 coals on bottom and 14 on top. When rolls are golden brown, remove from Dutch oven and serve. Makes 8 servings.

VARIATION: If you like gravy, try serving these with chicken or turkey gravy drizzled over top.

SHEPHERD'S PIE

Dutch oven size: 12-inch

2 pounds	**ground beef**
1	**medium onion,** chopped
2 cups	**string beans, peas,** or **corn** (or any combination)
2 cups	**cream of mushroom soup,** condensed
10	**potatoes cooked and mashed***
1 cup	**grated cheddar cheese**

Cook beef and onion in Dutch oven using 12–14 coals on bottom.
Drain grease and then add onion, beans, peas, corn, and soup. Spread
mashed potatoes over top and sprinkle with cheese. Bake 10 minutes at
350 degrees using 10 coals on bottom and 14 on top. Cheese should be
melted when done. Makes 12 servings.

*4 to 5 cups instant mashed potatoes may be substituted.

THE KING'S CHICKEN

Dutch oven size: 12-inch

1 tablespoon	**butter** or **margarine**
1/2 cup	**grated Monterey Jack cheese**
1/4 cup	**chopped fresh chives**
1/4 cup	**chopped parsley**
1 1/2 teaspoons	**salt**
1/2 teaspoon	**orange zest**
1/8 teaspoon	**pepper**
1/4 cup	**chopped fresh spinach**
2	**eggs**
1/2 cup	**orange juice**
4 tablespoons	**flour**
1 cup	**breadcrumbs**
1/2 teaspoon	**orange zest**
6	**boneless, skinless chicken breasts,** flattened to 1/4 inch thick
	Creamy White Mushroom Sauce (see Sauces, Soups, & Stews, page 81)

In a bowl, combine butter, cheese, herbs, salt, orange zest, pepper, and spinach, and then form into 6 finger-sized strips and chill until firm.

In a separate bowl, combine eggs, orange juice, and flour. Pour batter into Dutch oven. Heat and stir continually until slightly thickened. Remove from heat and set aside. Thoroughly mix breadcrumbs and orange zest and set aside.

Roll 1 filling finger in each flattened chicken breast and then secure with toothpick, if necessary. Dip in batter, then roll in breadcrumb mixture. Place in Dutch oven sprayed with nonstick spray. Bake 45 minutes at 350 degrees using 10 coals on bottom and 14 on top. Serve with Creamy White Mushroom Sauce over top. Makes 8–10 servings.

STUFFED FLANK STEAK

Dutch oven size: 14-inch

1- to 2-pound	**flank steak,** flattened to ¼ inch thick
	salt and pepper, to taste
¼ cup	**toasted pine nuts**
⅓ cup	**chopped mint**
½ cup	**chopped fresh parsley**
5	**cloves garlic,** crushed
¼ cup	**fresh grated Parmesan cheese**
1	**lemon,** juiced
2 tablespoons	**olive oil,** divided
1 to 2 cups	**Fresh Tomato Sauce** (see Sauces, Soups, & Stews, page 80)

Sprinkle steak with salt and pepper. Place in refrigerator to keep cold while preparing other items.

In a small bowl, combine nuts, mint, parsley, garlic, cheese, lemon juice, and 1 tablespoon oil. Stir together. Remove meat from refrigerator and spread mixture on meat. Roll meat up across the grain like a jelly roll and then tie with string to secure. Season with more salt and pepper.

In a warm Dutch oven using 18–20 coals on bottom, place remaining oil and sear steak on all sides. Pour Fresh Tomato Sauce over top. Bring to a boil, and then remove coals leaving 10–12 on bottom, and put 16–18 new coals on top to get a nice simmer. Cover Dutch oven and let simmer at 350 degrees for 60 minutes, turning steak a few times during cooking. Remove from heat and let sit 10–15 minutes. Cut into ½-inch strips and serve with Fresh Tomato Sauce poured over top. Makes 8 servings.

DUTCH OVEN LASAGNA

Dutch oven size: 14-inch

1 package (16 ounces)	**lasagna noodles**
1 1/2 pounds	**ground beef,** browned and drained
1	**large onion,** chopped
3	**cloves garlic,** minced
1 1/2 quarts	**spaghetti sauce**
1 carton (32 ounces)	**small curd cottage cheese**
2	**eggs,** well beaten
1 package (8 ounces)	**cream cheese,** softened
2 pounds	**grated mozzarella cheese**

Cook lasagna noodles according to package directions, then drain and set aside. In a bowl, combine browned beef with onion and garlic. Mix with spaghetti sauce.

In a separate bowl, mix cottage cheese, eggs, and cream cheese.

Layer half the sauce mixture, noodles, and cottage cheese mixture in Dutch oven. Repeat layers and then sprinkle cheese over top. Bake 45 minutes, or until cheese melts and is bubbly, at 350 degrees using 10 coals on bottom and 18 on top. Makes 16 servings.

SWEET & SOUR DUTCH OVEN

Dutch oven size: 12-inch

4 pounds	**beef, pork,** or **chicken,** cut into 1-inch chunks
4 pounds	**carrots,** sliced
1 tablespoon	**olive oil**
1 cup	**chopped onion**
4 pounds	**sliced mushrooms**
1 bottle (10 ounces)	**soy sauce**
1 bottle (24 ounces)	**ketchup**
1 1/2 cups	**sugar**
1/4 cup	**vinegar**
2 cans (20 ounces each)	**pineapple chunks,** juice reserved
2	**green bell peppers,** diced
	cornstarch

Stir fry meat and carrots in oil in Dutch oven until cooked through. Add onion and mushrooms. Cook until mushrooms are tender. Add enough water to cover bottom of oven. Add soy sauce, ketchup, sugar, vinegar, and pineapple juice. Stir together and bring to a boil. Bake 35–40 minutes at 375–400 degrees using 22–30 coals on bottom. Cook until the color of sauce is burnt orange. Add peppers and then cornstarch until it reaches desired thickness. Remove from heat and add pineapple. Serve meat and sauce over rice. Makes 12 servings.

CORNED BEEF MACARONI

Dutch oven size: 12-inch

I can (10.5 ounces)	**cream of mushroom soup,** condensed
I can (10.5 ounces)	**cream of chicken soup,** condensed
I cup	**milk**
I cup	**grated cheddar cheese**
I can (12 ounces)	**corned beef**
2 cups	**dry macaroni,** cooked and drained
	salt and pepper, to taste

Mix all ingredients together in Dutch oven and bake 30–40 minutes, or until hot and bubbly, at 350 degrees using 10 coals on bottom and 14 on top. Season with salt and pepper and stir before serving. Makes 6–8 servings.

DUTCH OVEN MUTTON

Dutch oven size: 12-inch

    1 to 1 1/2 cups **olive oil**
        4 to 6 **mutton chops,** approximately 1/2 to 3/4 inch thick
    1 teaspoon **season salt**

Pour oil in Dutch oven and heat to almost boiling at 400 degrees using 28 coals on bottom. Lay chops on plate, and sprinkle with season salt. Place chops in oil and cook 2 minutes on each side, or until done and fat is crisp. Makes 4–6 servings.

CATALINA CHICKEN

Dutch oven size: 12-inch

3 to 4 pounds **chicken leg and thigh pieces,** skinned*
1 bottle (24 ounces) **Catalina salad dressing**

Layer chicken in Dutch oven. Pour dressing over top and bake 60 minutes, or until chicken falls off bones, at 350 degrees using 10 coals on bottom and 14 on top. Makes 8–10 servings.

*Boneless, skinless chicken breasts may be substituted.

HAMBURGER RICE CASSEROLE

Dutch oven size: 12-inch

1 pound	**ground beef**
1	**medium onion,** chopped
1 cup	**uncooked white rice**
2 cups	**water**
1/4 cup	**soy sauce**
1 can (10.5 ounces)	**cream of mushroom soup,** condensed
1 can (10.5 ounces)	**cream of chicken soup,** condensed

Brown beef and onion in Dutch oven using 20–24 coals on bottom.
Add remaining ingredients and bake 60–90 minutes at 350 degrees
using 10 coals on bottom and 14 on top. Check to see if rice is cooked
through and stir before serving. Makes 8 servings.

SLOPPY JOES

Dutch oven size: 12-inch

1 pound	**ground beef**
1 can (10.75 ounces)	**chicken gumbo soup,** condensed
$1/2$ cup	**ketchup**
$1/8$ cup	**mustard**
$1/2$	**medium onion,** chopped
1 can (8 ounces)	**tomato sauce**
2 tablespoons	**Worcestershire sauce**
	hamburger buns

In Dutch oven, brown hamburger using 30 coals on bottom. Drain and then add remaining ingredients except hamburger buns. Remove enough coals from bottom to achieve a simmer. Cover and simmer for 30 minutes, stirring occasionally to prevent burning. Serve on hamburger buns. Makes 4–6 servings.

MANICOTTI

Dutch oven size: 10-inch, 12-inch

1 envelope **spaghetti sauce mix**
1 pound **ground beef**
$1/4$ pound **grated asiago** (or other sharp cheese)
1 can (8 ounces) **tomato sauce**
1 package (8 ounces) **uncooked manicotti noodles**
$1/2$ pound **grated Monterey Jack cheese**

In 10-inch Dutch oven using 10 coals on bottom, make spaghetti sauce mix according to package directions and gently simmer.

Brown beef in 12-inch Dutch oven using 12–14 coals on bottom. Place in a bowl to cool. Mix asiago cheese in browned beef and then add tomato sauce. Stuff into manicotti noodles. Put enough spaghetti sauce in the bottom of 12-inch Dutch oven just to cover. Place stuffed manicotti over top. Spoon any leftover beef mixture over top, followed by remaining spaghetti sauce. Cover with cheese. Bake 40–45 minutes, or until manicotti shells are soft, at 350 degrees using 10 coals on bottom and 14 on top. Makes 4–6 servings.

APRICOT-RASPBERRY GLAZED CORNISH HENS

Dutch oven size: 14-inch, deep

I can (11.5 ounces)	**apricot nectar**
3 to 5	**Cornish hens**
I cup	**raspberry vinaigrette dressing**
I cup	**apricot jam**
I tablespoon	**volcano seasoning***
	salt and pepper, to taste
	rosemary sprigs

Inject apricot nectar into breasts of hens 24 hours before cooking and refrigerate.

In a bowl, mix dressing and jam together and set aside.

Preheat Dutch oven to 450 degrees using 22 coals on bottom and 23 on top. Wash hens and season with volcano seasoning, salt, and pepper. Place 1 or 2 sprigs of rosemary inside each hen. Place hens on a rack in Dutch oven. Bake 45–60 minutes, reducing heat as hens brown, to prevent burning. Glaze with dressing mixture about 20 minutes before finished cooking. Remove rosemary sprigs, and then glaze again just before serving. Makes 6–8 servings.

*Volcano seasoning is found anywhere volcano cookers are sold, such as Sportsman's Warehouse.

EASY CHICKEN AND RICE

Dutch oven size: 14-inch

2 cups	**uncooked white rice**
2 cans (10.5 ounces each)	**cream of chicken, mushroom,** or **celery soup,** condensed
4 cups	**water**
4 to 6	**boneless, skinless chicken breasts**
1 envelope	**onion soup mix**
	grated cheddar cheese

Stir together rice, cream soups, and water until well blended in Dutch oven. Place chicken over rice mixture and sprinkle with dry soup mix. Bake 60 minutes at 350 degrees using 10 coals on bottom and 18 on top. Sprinkle desired amount of cheese over top and let melt before serving. Makes 4–6 servings.

CHILI VERDE

Dutch oven size: 12-inch

6	**pork chops,** cut into 1 inch pieces
1/2 pound	**ground beef**
2 tablespoons	**olive oil**
1	**onion,** chopped
1	**clove garlic,** chopped
3 cans (4 ounces each)	**chopped green chiles**
2 cans (14.5 ounces each)	**stewed tomatoes**
1	**jalapeno,** chopped
1/2 teaspoon	**salt**
1/8 teaspoon	**fresh ground black pepper**
3 cups	**grated cheddar cheese**
16	**medium flour tortillas**

In Dutch oven, brown pork and beef using oil. Add onion, garlic, green chiles, and stewed tomatoes. Add jalapeno. Bake 45–60 minutes at 350 degrees using 10 coals on bottom and 14 on top, stirring. Serve in warm flour tortillas. Makes 8 servings.

SAUSAGE-ZUCCHINI RICE CASSEROLE

Dutch oven size: 12-inch

2 cups	**uncooked white rice**
1 cup	**chopped celery**
1	**large onion**, chopped
1 pound	**sausage,** browned and drained
4 cubes	**beef bouillon,** dissolved in water
4 cups	**warm water** (for the bouillon)
1 can (10.5 ounces)	**cream of chicken soup,** condensed
1 cup	**chopped zucchini**

Layer rice, celery, onion, sausage, bouillon mixture, soup, and zucchini in Dutch oven sprayed with nonstick spray. Bake 60 minutes at 375 degrees using 10 coals on bottom and 16 on top. Stir prior to serving. Makes 8 servings.

SIDE DISHES

CABBAGE ROLLS

Dutch oven size: 12-inch

1 1/2 pounds	**ground beef**
1	**large head cabbage**
1	**medium onion,** finely chopped
2 tablespoons	**melted butter** or **oil**
1 cup	**uncooked short grain rice**
1/4 cup	**water**
1/2 teaspoon	**allspice**
	salt and pepper, to taste
4	**cloves garlic,** finely chopped and divided
1/4 cup	**lemon juice**

In Dutch oven, brown beef, then drain and set aside. Wipe out Dutch oven with a paper towel. Core cabbage and remove leaves carefully. Boil leaves in salted water until limp and then drain. Wipe Dutch oven dry with paper towel. Fry onion in butter or oil until translucent. Add cooked beef, rice, water, allspice, salt, and pepper. Combine thoroughly.

Place a tablespoon of beef mixture on bottom edge of a cabbage leaf and roll, tucking sides like an egg roll to contain filling. Place rolls seam-side down and close together. Sprinkle with garlic and lemon juice. If more than one layer, sprinkle each layer.

Add enough water to just cover rolls. Bring to a simmer using 24 coals on bottom. Once simmer is achieved, cover and simmer 60 minutes. Makes 6 servings.

POTATOES, ONION, AND BACON

Dutch oven size: 12-inch

1/2 to 1 pound **bacon,** cut into 1-inch pieces
1 **medium onion,** sliced
6 to 8 **red potatoes,** sliced
salt and pepper, to taste

Cook bacon in Dutch oven, using 20–24 coals on bottom. Add onion when bacon is almost cooked. After bacon is crisp, remove all coals. Add potatoes, salt, and pepper. Bake 90 minutes at 350 degrees, using 10 new coals on bottom and 14 new on top, stirring every 10–15 minutes. Pay attention to how tender the potatoes are because you don't want to overcook them. Makes 8 servings.

HONEY-GLAZED CARROTS

Dutch oven size: 10-inch

$^1/_4$ cup **butter** or **margarine**
1 pound **baby carrots**
$^1/_2$ cup **honey**
2 tablespoons **brown sugar**

Place butter in warm Dutch oven and melt. Add carrots to melted butter, and then pour honey over top and sprinkle with brown sugar. Cover and bake 30 minutes, or until tender, at 325 degrees using 8 coals on bottom and 10 on top. Makes 6 servings.

CORN ON THE COB

Dutch oven size: 12-inch

6 **cobs fresh sweet corn,** still in husks
$^1/_2$ cup **water**

Trim ends of corn and husks. Remove outer husk layer, leaving two inner layers. Pull inner layers back slightly to remove silk. Fold husk back over corn.

In Dutch oven with a rack, pour in water and bring to a boil using 30 coals on bottom. Layer husk-covered corn on the rack, cover, and let steam 10–20 minutes, or until corn is fork tender. Remove and serve warm. Makes 6 servings.

CHEESY POTATOES

Dutch oven size: 12-inch, 12-inch

6	**large potatoes***
$^1/_4$ cup	**butter** or **margarine,** melted
1 pint	**sour cream**
1 can (10.5 ounces)	**cream of chicken soup,** condensed
$^1/_4$ cup	**chopped onion**
4 cups	**grated cheddar cheese**

In one 12-inch Dutch oven, boil potatoes, cool, remove from oven, and then grate. Empty water from oven and then add butter, sour cream, soup, and onion. Simmer 5 minutes.

In second 12-inch Dutch oven, layer a third of sauce, potatoes, and cheese. Repeat layers until all ingredients are used, finishing with a layer of cheese. Bake 20 minutes at 350 degrees using 10 coals on bottom and 14 on top. Makes 12 servings.

*1 bag frozen shredded hash browns, thawed, may be substituted. Do not boil hash browns if using.

DUTCH OVEN POTATOES

Dutch oven size: 12-inch

1 pound	**bacon,** cut into 1-inch pieces
10	**medium russet potatoes,** peeled and thinly sliced
5	**carrots,** thinly sliced (optional)
2	**medium onions,** peeled and diced
	salt and pepper, to taste
1 can (10.5 ounces)	**cream of mushroom soup,** condensed
1 container (24 ounces)	**sour cream**
1 package (8 ounces)	**sliced mushrooms**
1 pound	**grated cheddar cheese**

Brown bacon pieces in Dutch oven using 10–12 coals on bottom. Stir frequently to prevent burning. When done, remove and set aside. Drain half the grease from oven, then add potatoes, carrots, and onions. Stir well and add enough water to cover 1 inch in bottom of oven. Season with salt and pepper. Cover and bake 35–40 minutes, or until potatoes are tender, at 350 degrees using 10 coals on bottom and 14 on top. Stir in soup, sour cream, mushrooms, and bacon. Bake 10 minutes more. Sprinkle cheese over top and cover until cheese melts. Makes 12–14 servings.

Sauces, Soups, & Stews

FRESH TOMATO SAUCE

Dutch oven size: 12-inch

2 tablespoons	**olive oil**
4 to 8	**cloves garlic,** crushed
$^1/_4$	**medium onion,** finely chopped
1	**tomato,** cored and chopped
1 can (14 ounces)	**Italian stewed tomatoes**
$^1/_4$ cup	**chopped fresh parsley**
1 can (14 ounces)	**chicken broth**
$^1/_2$ teaspoon	**dried marjoram**
$^1/_2$ teaspoon	**dried rosemary,** crushed
1 $^1/_2$ tablespoons	**butter** or **margarine**
	salt and pepper, to taste

Heat Dutch oven to 350 degrees using 18–20 coals on bottom. Add oil, garlic, and onion. Saute until onion is translucent. Add remaining ingredients except butter, salt, and pepper. Bring to a boil and then remove enough coals to get a gentle simmer and cook about 60 minutes, stirring occasionally. Stir in butter, salt, and pepper. This sauce is great over chicken, pork, or pasta. Makes 2 cups.

80

CREAMY WHITE MUSHROOM SAUCE

Dutch oven size: 10-inch

1 package (8 ounces)	**sliced mushrooms**
3 tablespoons	**flour**
3 tablespoons	**butter** or **margarine**
$1/2$ cup	**chicken broth**
1 cup	**light cream** or **whipping cream**
$1/4$ cup	**pimientos**
2 teaspoons	**Dijon mustard**

Place mushrooms in large zipper-lock bag and sprinkle flour over top, and then shake to coat. Melt butter in Dutch oven then add mushrooms and saute using 10 coals on bottom for 5 minutes, or until mushrooms are tender. Add broth and cream and stir until thickened. Add pimientos and mustard. Makes 2 cups.

CREAMY PARMESAN SAUCE

Dutch oven size: 8-inch

1 can (10.75 ounces)	**cream of mushroom soup,** condensed
1 cup	**milk**
2 tablespoons	**chopped fresh parsley**
$^1/_2$ cup	**butter** or **margarine**
$^3/_4$ cup	**grated fresh parmesan cheese**

In Dutch oven, blend soup, milk, and parsley. Add butter and simmer using 6 coals on bottom. Stir frequently until butter melts and mixture is heated through. Add cheese and stir until melted. Makes 2 cups.

GOOD OL' DUTCH OVEN CHILI

Dutch oven size: 12-inch

1 pound	**ground beef**
1 1/2 cups	**chopped onion**
1 1/2 cups	**chopped green bell pepper**
1 can (29 ounces)	**Italian stewed tomatoes**
1 can (16 ounces)	**tomato sauce**
1 can (15.25 ounces)	**corn,** drained
5 tablespoons	**Worcestershire sauce**
2 teaspoons	**chili powder**
1 teaspoon	**garlic powder**
1 can (32 ounces)	**red beans,** rinsed and drained

In Dutch oven, brown beef, onion, and bell pepper using 30 coals on bottom. Add remaining ingredients and remove enough coals from bottom to achieve a simmer. Let simmer 35–40 minutes, stirring often. Makes 10 servings

WHITE CHILI

Dutch oven size: 12-inch

1 pound	**dry white beans**
4 tablespoons	**butter** or **margarine**
1	**medium onion,** diced
4 tablespoons	**chicken bouillon granules**
2 tablespoons	**salt**
8 to 10 cups	**water** (plus enough to cover beans)
2 cans (6.5 ounces each)	**chunk chicken**
2 cans (4 ounces each)	**diced green chiles**
1 container (16 ounces)	**sour cream**

Rinse beans, cover with water and set aside. Melt butter in Dutch oven using 10 coals on bottom. Add onion and cook until translucent. Drain beans and add to onion with bouillon, salt, and 8 cups water. Cover and cook 2–3 hours, or until beans are tender, using 30–40 coals on bottom. Add chicken and chiles and cook 30 minutes more. Add sour cream and simmer until serving time. Check water level often and add more water as needed. Remove enough coals to achieve simmer. Makes 12–14 servings.

DUTCH OVEN STEW

Dutch oven size: 12-inch

I pound	**beef stew meat**
I	**medium onion,** chopped
2 cans (10.5 ounces each)	**cream of mushroom** or **chicken soup,** condensed
I to 2 soup cans	**water**
2 cups	**sliced celery**
2 cups	**sliced carrots**
6	**potatoes,** cut into cubes
I can (14.5 ounces)	**whole kernel corn,** with liquid
I can (14.5 ounces)	**whole green beans,** with liquid

Brown beef in bottom of Dutch oven at 350 degrees using 10 coals on bottom and 14 on top. Add onion, soup, and 1 can water for a thick stew or 2 cans water for thin. Add vegetables and cook 60 minutes. Makes 10–12 servings.

KVETCHER STEW

Dutch oven size: 12-inch

2 pounds	**stew meat,** cut in 1-inch cubes
8	**medium potatoes,** quartered
1 cup	**frozen kernel corn**
4 to 6	**carrots,** sliced
2	**medium onions,** coarsely chopped
4	**medium tomatoes,** diced
2	**cloves garlic,** finely chopped
1	**green bell pepper,** diced
top 4 inches	**celery stalk,** sliced (leaves included)
3 to 4	**bay leaves**
1 tablespoon	**beef bouillon**
1 cup	**water**

Brown meat in Dutch oven at 350 degrees using 10 coals on bottom and 14 on top. Add remaining ingredients and cover. Check every 20 minutes and stir. Stew is done when potatoes are soft, about 60–90 minutes. Makes 14–16 servings.

LAMB STEW

Dutch Oven Size: 12-inch

1 to 2 pounds	**fresh lamb**
1 cup	**chopped onion**
2 to 3	**cloves garlic,** chopped
4 cups	**water**
1 cup	**carrots,** sliced
1 can (15.25 ounces)	**whole kernel corn,** drained
1 cup	**chopped celery**
1 cup	**fresh green beans**
2 cups	**cubed potatoes** (about 1 inch)
4 to 8	**beef bouillon cubes***

In a preheated Dutch Oven brown lamb along with onion and garlic. Add the water then add all of the remaining ingredients, except bouillon. Bring to a boil, add bouillon. Remove enough coals to get a good simmer. Simmer the stew for 45–60 minutes at 350 degrees using 10 coals on bottom 14 on top.

*Substitute teaspoons for cubes if using granules.

TORTILLA SOUP

Dutch oven size: 12-inch

4 tablespoons	**olive oil**
24	**corn tortillas**
1	**large onion,** chopped
3	**cloves garlic,** finely chopped
1	**red bell pepper,** chopped
4	**yellow wax peppers,** chopped
4	**boneless, skinless chicken breasts,** cut into chunks
3 quarts	**water**
2 tablespoons	**Persil Chile powder***
2 tablespoons	**New Mexico Chile powder***
2 tablespoons	**California Chile powder***
2 cans (16 ounces each)	**tomatoes**
1 tablespoon	**salt**
1 pound	**grated Monterey Jack cheese**
4	**avocados,** cut into bite-size chunks

Heat Dutch oven to 375 degrees using 10–13 coals on bottom and add enough oil to cover bottom. Cut tortillas into 1-inch squares. Place tortillas squares, one handful at a time, in hot oil and fry until brown. Drain oil from tortillas using paper towel and then set tortillas aside.

Saute onion, garlic, bell pepper, and yellow peppers in hot oil. Add chicken and brown. Add water, chile powders, tomatoes, and salt. Place 13 coals on top of Dutch oven, leaving 13 on bottom that were used earlier. Let simmer 15 minutes. Just before serving, add tortilla squares to soup. Put cheese in bottom of bowls and ladle soup into bowls. Garnish with avocados over top. Makes 15–20 servings.

*Persil, New Mexico, and California chile powders can be found at any specialty store, and in some large chain grocery stores.

CHUNKY CHICKEN SOUP

Dutch oven size: 12-inch

1 bottle (24 ounces)	**ketchup**
2 cans (12 ounces each)	**cola**
6	**boneless, skinless chicken breasts,** cut into 1 inch cubes
6	**large russet potatoes,** cut into $^1/_2$-inch cubes
8	**large carrots,** sliced $^1/_2$ inch thick
1 cup	**uncooked long grain rice**

In Dutch oven, mix together ketchup and cola. Add chicken and vegetables and then cover. Simmer 60–90 minutes using 10 coals on the bottom. Makes 8 servings.

VARIATION: If you prefer a thinner soup, gradually add water until desired consistency is reached.

HAMBURGER SOUP

Dutch oven size: 12-inch

1 pound	**ground beef**
1 cup	**chopped onion**
1 cup	**chopped green bell pepper**
1 can (29 ounces)	**Italian stewed tomatoes**
1 can (16 ounces)	**tomato sauce**
1 can (15.25 ounces)	**whole kernel corn,** drained (optional)
5 tablespoons	**Worcestershire sauce**
2 teaspoons	**chili powder**
1 teaspoon	**garlic powder**
1 can (32 ounces)	**red beans,** rinsed and drained
8 cups	**water**
3	**carrots,** sliced
3	**russet potatoes,** cut into 1 inch cubes
4	**celery stalks,** sliced
1	**bay leaf**

In Dutch oven, brown beef, onion, and bell pepper using 30 coals on bottom. Drain and add remaining ingredients. Bring to a boil, and then remove enough coals from bottom to achieve a simmer. Cover and simmer 60 minutes, stirring often. Remove bay leaf before serving. Makes 12–16 servings.

DESSERTS

RASPBERRY-PEACH PIE

Dutch oven size: 12-inch

1 1/2 cups	**sugar**
7 tablespoons	**Clear-Jell**
6 to 8	**peaches,** peeled and sliced
2 cups	**raspberries**
2 teaspoons	**almond extract**
1/2 cup	**red wine**
2 cups	**shortening**
4 cups	**flour**
1 cup	**hot water**
1/2 teaspoon	**salt**
2 tablespoons	**butter** or **margarine,** cubed
1/4 cup	**milk**

In a large bowl, mix sugar and Clear-Jell. Add fruit, almond extract, and wine. Stir gently, just enough to combine.

In a separate bowl, cut shortening into flour with a pastry cutter until crumbly. Add water and salt and gently toss with a fork just enough to moisten. Knead dough until uniform in texture, and then divide into 2 balls. Roll 1 out to a 1/4-inch-thick circle on a floured surface. Fold dough in half and gently place in bottom of Dutch oven sprayed with nonstick spray. Unfold dough, making sure it covers the bottom and halfway up sides of oven. Carefully spoon fruit mixture into crust. Place cubes of butter over fruit mixture. Roll out second dough ball for top crust, cutting a few slits for venting. Place crust over filling and seal the bottom and top crust edges with water. Brush top crust with milk. Bake 50–60 minutes, or until done, at 350 degrees using 10 coals on bottom and 14–16 on top. Makes 8 servings.

CHERRY PIE

Dutch oven size: 12-inch

3 cups	**flour**
1 1/2 teaspoons	**sugar**
1 1/2 teaspoons	**salt**
3/4 teaspoon	**baking powder**
1 1/2 cups	**shortening**
3/4 cup	**ice water**
1	**egg**
2 tablespoons	**water**
3 1/2 cups	**sugar**
2 teaspoons	**Fruit Fresh**
3/4 cup	**Clear-Jell**
8 cups	**pitted pie cherries and juice**
2 teaspoons	**almond extract**

In a bowl, mix flour, sugar, salt, and baking powder together. Cut shortening in with a pastry cutter, then stir in 3/4 cup water slowly. Roll out three-fourths of dough and then press in bottom and halfway up the sides of chilled Dutch oven sprayed with nonstick spray. Combine egg and 2 tablespoons water, then coat bottom crust with egg wash.

In a separate bowl, mix sugar, Fruit Fresh, and Clear-Jell together and pour over cherries. Slightly mash cherries as you stir and then add almond extract. Pour fruit mixture into piecrust. Roll remaining dough out and place over filling. Seal bottom and top crust edges with water. Form a decorative edge, if desired, and coat with remaining egg wash. Bake 60–80 minutes, or until done, at 400 degrees using 12–15 coals on bottom and 20 on top. Makes 8 servings.

PECAN PIE

Dutch oven size: 10-inch

4	**eggs**
1 1/3 cups	**sugar**
1 1/3 cups	**corn syrup***
4 tablespoons	**butter** or **margarine,** melted
1 1/2 teaspoons	**vanilla**
1 1/3 cups	**chopped pecans**
1	**refrigerated piecrust**

In a bowl, beat eggs with a fork. Add sugar and mix well, and then stir in corn syrup. Add butter and vanilla and mix well. Stir in pecans. Press piecrust in bottom of Dutch oven sprayed with nonstick spray. Spoon filling into crust. Bake 65–75 minutes, or until done, at 400 degrees using 8 coals on bottom and 15 on top. To check doneness of pie, insert a knife in center. If it comes out with a clear shiny coating, it is done. Makes 8 servings.

*Light corn syrup gives it a lighter taste and color. Dark corn syrup gives it a rich taste and darker color.

LEMON HEADS PIE

Dutch oven size: 12-inch

6$^1/_2$ cups	**flour,** divided
1$^1/_2$ teaspoons	**salt**
1$^2/_3$ cups	**shortening**
1$^3/_4$ cups	**cold water,** divided
3 packages (8 ounces each)	**cream cheese**
2$^1/_2$ cups plus 1 teaspoon	**sugar,** divided
$^1/_4$ cup	**butter** or **margarine,** softened
6	**eggs**
$^1/_8$ teaspoon	**salt**
2	**lemons**
$^1/_2$ cup	**Lemon Heads candy,** crushed
1	**egg white,** whipped
$^1/_2$ teaspoon	**cinnamon**

In a bowl, mix 5 cups flour and 1$^1/_2$ teaspoons salt together. Cut in shortening with a pastry cutter until crumbly. Add 1$^1/_4$ cups water gradually and mix until dough holds together. Cover and set aside.

In a separate bowl, mix cream cheese, 2$^1/_2$ cups sugar, and butter. Add eggs and mix well, then stir in remaining flour and salt. Zest 1 lemon and add to cream cheese mixture. Peel and slice remaining lemon paper-thin. Add to mixture with remaining water. Stir in candy and set aside.

Line Dutch oven with parchment paper so it's easier to remove the cooked pie. Roll out half the dough and press into bottom of Dutch oven. Pour filling into crust. Roll out remaining dough and place over filling. Seal bottom and top crust edges with water, and cut slits to vent steam. Brush egg white over top, and then sprinkle remaining sugar and cinnamon over top. Bake 35–45 minutes, or until golden brown, at 400 degrees using 12 coals on bottom and 18 on top. Remove from heat, then remove from oven when cooled enough to do so without falling apart. Cool completely on wire rack. Makes 8 servings.

PEAR-RASPBERRY PIE

Dutch oven size: 12-inch

4 cups	**flour**
2 cups	**shortening**
$3/4$ teaspoon	**salt,** divided
1 cup	**hot water**
1 cup	**sugar**
3 to $3^1/2$ tablespoons	**quick-cooking tapioca**
$1/4$ teaspoon	**ground nutmeg**
5 to 6	**pears,** peeled and sliced
2 tablespoons	**amaretto**
1 can (21 ounces)	**raspberry pie filling**
$1/4$ cup	**milk**

In a bowl, cut flour, shortening, and $1/2$ teaspoon salt together with a pastry cutter until crumbly. Add water gradually and gently toss with a fork just until moist. Knead dough a few times until uniform in texture. Divide into 2 balls. Roll 1 out to a $1/4$-inch-thick circle on a floured surface. Fold dough in half and place in Dutch oven sprayed with nonstick spray. It should cover bottom and just over halfway up the sides of oven.

In a separate bowl, combine sugar, tapioca, remaining salt, and nutmeg. Add pears and toss to coat. Sprinkle amaretto evenly over coated pears. Place pears in bottom crust, and then spoon pie filling over top. Roll out second dough ball to create top crust and cut slits for venting. Place over filling and seal bottom and top crust edges with water. Brush milk over top. Bake 50–60 minutes, or until crust is golden brown and filling is bubbling, at 350 degrees using 10 coals on bottom and 14 on top. Makes 8 servings.

CHOCOLATE CAKE

Dutch oven size: 12-inch Camp Chef Ultimate

3 cups	**flour**
1 cup plus 2 tablespoons	**cocoa**
3 teaspoons	**baking soda**
$3/4$ teaspoon	**baking powder**
$3/4$ teaspoon	**salt**
$1^{1}/_4$ cups	**butter** or **margarine,** softened
$3^{1}/_4$ cups	**sugar,** divided
3	**eggs**
$1^{1}/_2$ teaspoons	**vanilla**
$1^{1}/_2$ cups	**buttermilk***
1 cup plus 2 tablespoons	**sour cream**
1 package (8 ounces)	**cream cheese,** softened
2 tablespoons	**milk**
1 container (12 ounces)	**whipped topping,** thawed
1 small box	**instant chocolate pudding mix,** sifted

In a bowl, sift together flour, cocoa, baking soda, baking powder, and salt and set aside.

In a separate bowl, cream butter and 3 cups sugar until well blended, then beat in eggs and vanilla. Alternately add buttermilk, sour cream, and flour mixture, stirring after each addition. Pour into Dutch oven sprayed with nonstick spray. Bake 70–80 minutes at 350 degrees using 9 coals on bottom and 16 on top.

While baking, mix together cream cheese, milk, and remaining sugar. Fold in whipped topping and pudding mix. Frost the cake when cooled and serve. Makes 12 servings.

*Make your own buttermilk by combining $1/4$ cup lemon juice with $1^{1}/_4$ cups milk.

BANANA CAKE

Dutch oven size: 12-inch

$^2/_3$ cup	**sugar**
$^1/_3$ cup	**shortening**
2	**eggs**
3 tablespoons	**buttermilk***
4 to 5	**bananas,** overripe and mashed
2 cups	**flour**
$^1/_2$ teaspoon	**baking soda**
1 teaspoon	**baking powder**
$^1/_2$ teaspoon	**salt**
$^1/_2$ cup	**chocolate chips**

In a small bowl, cream sugar and shortening together. Add eggs, buttermilk, and bananas. Mix in flour, baking soda, baking powder, salt, and chocolate chips. Mix until well blended and smooth. Pour mixture into Dutch oven sprayed with nonstick spray. Bake 35–40 minutes at 350 degrees using 10 coals on bottom and 14 on top. Makes 12 servings.

*Make your own buttermilk by combining 3 tablespoons milk with 1 teaspoon lemon juice.

BERRY-PEACH COBBLER

Dutch oven size: 12-inch

> 1 can (29 ounces) **peach halves** or **slices,** liquid reserved
> 1 can (21 ounces) **raspberry pie filling**
> 1 **yellow cake mix**

Drain juice from peaches and set aside. Place peach halves in bottom of Dutch oven, reserving 3–4 slices. Cut reserved slices into small pieces, and then mix with 4 teaspoons pie filling. Spoon remaining pie filling over peaches in bottom of oven.

In a bowl, make cake batter according to package directions, eliminating the eggs and using peach juice in place of water. If not enough juice, add water to make up difference. Add peach and pie filling mixture to batter. Pour batter over fruit in bottom of oven. Bake 30–35 minutes, or until it begins to pull away from sides, at 350 degrees using 10 coals on bottom and 14 on top. Makes 12 servings.

DUMP COBBLER

Dutch oven size: 12-inch

1 can (21 ounces)	**apple pie filling**
1	**spice cake mix**
1 can	**Dr. Pepper** or **lemon-lime soda***

Spoon pie filling in bottom of Dutch oven, then sprinkle cake mix over top. Pour soda over cake mix, trying to completely cover. Bake at 350 degrees using 10 coals on bottom and 14 on top. Bake 30–35 minutes, or until cake begins pulling away from sides. Makes 12 servings.

*Do not use diet soda.

SOUTHERN-STYLE PEACH COBBLER

Dutch oven size: 12-inch

2 cups	**flour**
2 cups	**sugar**
2 cups	**evaporated milk**
1 cup	**butter** or **margarine,** melted
2 cans (29 ounces each)	**peaches,** juice reserved

In a bowl, combine flour, sugar, evaporated milk, butter, and 1/2 cup reserved peach juice until smooth. Place peaches in bottom of Dutch oven sprayed with nonstick spray. Pour batter over top. Bake at 350 degrees using 10 coals on bottom and 14 on top. Bake 30–35 minutes, or until golden brown. Serve warm. Makes 12 servings.

APPLE SPICE CAKE

Dutch oven size: 12-inch, 10-inch

1	**spice cake mix**
1 1/4 cups	**water**
1/3 cup	**vegetable oil**
3	**egg whites**
2 cans (21 ounces each)	**apple pie filling**

Sauce:

1 1/2 cups	**light brown sugar**
3/4 cup	**light corn syrup**
4 tablespoons	**butter** or **margarine**
1/2 cup	**light cream**

In a large bowl, combine cake mix, water, oil, and egg whites and then set aside. Place parchment paper in bottom of 12-inch Dutch oven. Pour pie filling over parchment paper. Pour batter over pie filling. Bake at 375 degrees using 8 coals on bottom and 18 on top. Bake 25–35 minutes, or until toothpick inserted in center comes out clean. Remove from Dutch oven by inverting onto cool 12-inch Dutch oven lid, and remove parchment paper.

In 10-inch Dutch oven, heat sugar, syrup, and butter over low heat, using 10 coals. Heat until mixture reaches a softball stage, and then add cream and heat 2 minutes more. Serve cake with sauce drizzled over top. Makes 12 servings.

CHOCOLATE PEPPERMINT CAKE

Dutch oven size: 12-inch

1 teaspoon	**salt**
3 cups	**sifted flour**
2 teaspoons	**baking soda**
4 heaping tablespoons	**cocoa**
2 cups	**sugar**
2 teaspoons	**vinegar**
10 tablespoons	**butter** or **margarine,** melted
$^1/_4$ teaspoon	**peppermint extract**
2 cups	**cold water**
$^3/_4$ cup	**semisweet chocolate chips**

Frosting:

$^1/_4$ teaspoon	**salt**
$^1/_4$ cup	**sugar**
2	**egg whites,** beaten
$^3/_4$ cup	**Karo syrup**
$1^1/_2$ tablespoons	**vanilla**
$^1/_8$ cup	**crushed peppermint candies**
$^1/_8$ cup	**Hershey's Chocolate syrup**

In a large bowl, sift salt, flour, baking soda, cocoa, and sugar together and set aside. In another bowl, combine vinegar, butter, peppermint extract, and water. Add to dry ingredients and stir until smooth. Stir in chocolate chips and then pour into Dutch oven sprayed with nonstick spray containing flour. Bake 30 minutes at 350 degrees using 10 coals on bottom and 14 on top, or until toothpick inserted in center comes out clean.

In a separate bowl, gradually add salt and sugar to beaten egg whites, beating until smooth. Slowly add Karo syrup and beat until stiff peaks form. Fold in vanilla. Frost cooled cake and sprinkle candies over top. Drizzle chocolate syrup over individual servings. Makes 12 servings.

DEVIL'S FOOD CAKE

Dutch oven size: 12-inch

2 **devil's food cake mixes**
1 package (12 ounces) **mini mint chips**
1 can (21 ounces) **cherry pie filling**

In a large bowl, prepare both cake mixes according to package directions. Fold in mint chips. Pour into Dutch oven sprayed with nonstick spray containing flour. Bake at 350 degrees using 10 coals on bottom and 14 on top. Bake 15–18 minutes, and then remove coals from bottom of oven. Place 8 more coals on top 45 minutes more, or until toothpick inserted in center comes out clean. Remove cake from Dutch oven and place on wire rack. When cake is completely cool, spoon pie filling over top. Makes 12 servings.

LEMON-ORANGE CAKE

Dutch oven size: 12-inch

1	**lemon cake mix**
1 box (3.4 ounces)	**vanilla instant pudding mix**
4	**eggs**
1/2 cup	**oil**
1 cup	**water**

Glaze:

2 teaspoons	**butter** or **margarine,** melted
1/2 cup	**orange juice**
3 cups	**powdered sugar**

In a bowl, combine cake mix, pudding mix, eggs, oil, and water and blend well. Pour batter into Dutch oven sprayed with nonstick spray containing flour. Bake at 350 degrees using 10 coals on bottom and 14 on top. Bake 30–35 minutes, or until toothpick inserted in center comes out clean.

In a separate bowl, mix butter, orange juice, and powdered sugar until smooth. Punch holes in top of cooled cake using handle of wooden spoon and pour glaze over top. Let sit 10–15 minutes before serving. Makes 12 servings.

PUMPKIN CRUMBLE

Dutch oven size: 12-inch

1 cup	**sugar**
1 1/2 teaspoons	**cinnamon**
1/2 teaspoon	**ginger**
1/2 teaspoon	**ground cloves**
1 can (12 ounces)	**evaporated milk**
1/2 teaspoon	**salt**
1/2 teaspoon	**nutmeg**
1/2 teaspoon	**allspice**
1 1/2 cups	**pumpkin** (not pumpkin pie filling)
2	**eggs**

Topping:

1/2 cup	**butter** or **margarine,** softened
1 1/2 cups	**sugar**
2 1/4 cups	**flour**
2 1/2 teaspoons	**baking powder**
1 teaspoon	**salt**

In a bowl, mix all the cake ingredients together until smooth. Pour batter into Dutch oven sprayed with nonstick spray.

In a separate bowl, combine butter, sugar, flour, baking powder, and salt until crumbly. Sprinkle over batter. Bake at 325 degrees using 8 coals on bottom and 16 on top. Bake 30–35 minutes, or until toothpick inserted in center comes out clean. After 30 minutes of baking, remove 3 coals from bottom and move to top so bottom of cake doesn't burn. Makes 12 servings.

SMACOS

Dutch oven size: 12-inch

1 teaspoon	**olive oil**
1 1/2 cups	**semi-sweet chocolate chips,**
	divided in 10 equal groups
10	**medium flour tortillas**
1 package (16 ounces)	**mini marshmallows,**
	divided in 10 equal groups

Using a paper towel, spread oil over bottom of Dutch oven. Heat Dutch oven using 10–14 coals on bottom. Place a tortilla in bottom of heated oven and layer one group chocolate chips and then one group marshmallows over top. Cover with lid for 1 minute. Remove lid and using a pair of tongs fold the tortilla in half, making a taco shape. Cover for another minute. Remove lid and then use tongs to place on a paper plate and cool. Repeat with remaining ingredients. Serve when cooled enough to handle. Makes 10 servings.

SWEET POACHED PEARS

Dutch oven size: 12-inch

6	**pears,** peeled and cored
1 tablespoon	**butter** or **margarine**
1/4 cup	**ginger ale**
25	**caramels,** unwrapped
25	**Red Hot Tamale candies**
1 box (8 ounces)	**Red Hots candies**

Place butter, ginger ale, caramels, and candies in warm Dutch oven and melt. Add more ginger ale as needed to cover bottom of oven to make poaching liquid 1/4 inch deep. Place pears in Dutch oven standing up. Cover and bake until fork-tender at 325 degrees using 10 coals on bottom and 13 on top. Baste pears with sauce as they are cooking. Carefully remove from Dutch oven and place on a cool Dutch oven lid. Drizzle sauce from the oven over pears and serve. Makes 6 servings.

S'MORES BROWNIES

Dutch oven size: 12-inch

1 cup	**butter** or **margarine,** melted
1/2 cup	**cocoa**
4	**eggs**
2 cups	**sugar**
1 teaspoon	**vanilla**
1 teaspoon	**cinnamon**
1/2 teaspoon	**salt**
1/2 teaspoon	**baking powder**
2 cups	**flour**
3/4 cup	**chopped pecans**
1 cup	**mini marshmallows**
1 cup	**chopped peanut butter cups**

In a bowl, whisk butter and cocoa together. Add eggs one at a time, whisking between each. Add sugar, vanilla, cinnamon, salt, baking powder, and flour. Pour into Dutch oven sprayed with nonstick spray containing flour. Sprinkle pecans over top. Bake at 400 degrees using 18 coals on bottom and 12 on top. Bake 12 minutes, and then remove heat from bottom, but continue baking with top heat 15–20 minutes more. Remove lid and sprinkle with marshmallows and peanut butter cups. Replace lid and remove all coals. Let sit 5–10 minutes before serving. Makes 12 servings.

WHITE CHOCOLATE-CARAMEL PECAN CHEESECAKE

Dutch oven size: 10-inch

7	**whole graham crackers**
1/4 cup	**butter** or **margarine,** cut up and softened
1 cup	**low-fat sour cream**
4	**eggs,** separated into yolks and whites
1/2 cup	**sugar**
1 tablespoon	**cornstarch**
3 packages (8 ounces each)	**low-fat cream cheese**
5 ounces	**white baking chocolate,** melted
2 tablespoons	**lemon juice**
2 tablespoons	**vanilla**
2 tablespoons	**hot fudge**
2 tablespoons	**caramel ice cream topping**
1/2 cup	**chopped pecans**
1/3 cup	**semisweet chocolate chips**

Place graham crackers in plastic zipper-lock bag and crush with rolling pin. Add butter and seal bag and then mush together with your hands. Press crust mixture in bottom and part way up the sides of Dutch oven lined with parchment paper. Blend sour cream, egg yolks, sugar, cornstarch, cream cheese, melted chocolate; lemon juice, and vanilla.

In a separate bowl, beat egg whites until stiff peaks form. Fold egg whites into cheesecake filling. Pour mixture over crust in Dutch oven. Bake at 325 degrees using 8 coals on bottom and 11 on top. Bake 45–60 minutes, or until center jiggles when lightly shaken. Let cool 60 minutes. Carefully remove from oven with liner. Garnish with hot fudge, caramel, pecans, and chocolate chips. Makes 12 servings.

CARROT CAKE

Dutch oven size: 14-inch

2 cups	**flour**
2 teaspoons	**baking soda**
1 teaspoon	**nutmeg**
2 teaspoons	**cinnamon**
1/2 teaspoon	**salt**
3	**eggs,** beaten
3/4 cup	**vegetable oil**
3/4 cup	**buttermilk***
2 cups	**sugar**
2 teaspoons	**vanilla extract**
1 can (8 ounces)	**crushed pineapple,** drained
2 cups	**grated carrots**
1 1/2 cups	**coconut**
1/2 cup	**raisins**
1 cup	**chopped pecans**
1 container	**cream cheese frosting**

Sift together first 5 ingredients and set aside.

In a bowl, beat eggs, oil, buttermilk, sugar, and vanilla. Add sifted dry ingredients, pineapple, carrots, coconut, raisins, and pecans. Pour batter into Dutch oven sprayed with nonstick spray containing flour. Bake at 350 degrees using 11 coals on bottom and 17 on top. Bake 55–65 minutes, or until toothpick inserted in center comes out clean. Remove from Dutch oven and place on wire rack until completely cool, and then frost. Makes 16 servings.

*Make your own buttermilk by combining 3/4 cup milk and 4 teaspoons lemon juice.

APPLE CINNAMON CAKE

Dutch oven size: 12-inch

2	**eggs**
1/2 teaspoon plus 1 pinch	**salt**
1 1/2 cups	**sugar**
2 3/4 teaspoons	**vanilla extract,** divided
1 cup	**vegetable oil**
2 tablespoons	**lemon juice**
1 tablespoon	**lemon zest**
3 heaping cups	**flour**
1 3/4 teaspoon	**cinnamon,** divided
1 1/4 teaspoons	**baking soda**
1/4 teaspoon	**nutmeg**
3 to 4	**Granny Smith apples,** peeled, cored, and grated (about 3 cups)
1 package (8 ounces)	**cream cheese,** softened
3/4 cup	**butter** or **margarine,** softened
4 cups	**powdered sugar**
	sliced almonds, for garnish

In a large bowl, beat together eggs, 1/2 teaspoon salt, sugar, 2 teaspoons vanilla, oil, lemon juice, and lemon zest and set aside.

In a separate bowl, combine flour, 1 teaspoon cinnamon, baking soda, and nutmeg. Gradually mix into the egg mixture and then stir in apples.

Pour batter into Dutch oven sprayed with nonstick spray containing flour. Bake at 350 degrees using 10 coals on bottom and 14 on top. Bake 75 minutes, or until toothpick inserted in center comes out clean. Remove cake from Dutch oven and cool.

In a bowl, combine all remaining ingredients except powdered sugar and almonds. Add powdered sugar 1 cup at a time and beat until smooth. Frost cooled cake and sprinkle almonds over top. Makes 12 servings.

ZUCCHINI-CARROT CAKE

Dutch oven size: 12-inch Camp Chef Ultimate

1/2 cup	**oil**
2 cups	**sugar**
3	**eggs**
3 teaspoons	**vanilla**
2 cups	**shredded zucchini**
I cup	**shredded carrots**
I can (8 ounces)	**crushed pineapple,** with liquid
I teaspoon	**salt**
I tablespoon	**cinnamon**
1/4 teaspoon	**baking powder**
I teaspoon	**baking soda**
3 cups	**flour**
1/2 cup	**chopped walnuts**

Frosting:

I package (8 ounces)	**cream cheese,** softened
1/2 cup	**butter** or **margarine,** softened
I teaspoon	**vanilla**
4 cups	**powdered sugar**

In a large bowl, cream oil, sugar, eggs, and vanilla. Stir in zucchini and carrots, then add pineapple and mix well. Add salt, cinnamon, baking powder, baking soda, and flour. Fold in nuts. Pour batter into Dutch oven sprayed with nonstick spray containing flour. Bake at 350 degrees using 10 coals on bottom and 14 on top. Bake 40–50 minutes, or until toothpick inserted in center comes out clean.

In a bowl, combine cream cheese and butter until smooth. Stir in vanilla, and then powdered sugar I cup at a time until well blended. Frost cooled cake and serve. Makes 12 servings.

APPLE CRUNCH

Dutch oven size: 12-inch

15 to 16 **apples,** peeled and sliced
1 cup **sugar**
1 cup **water**
1 tablespoon **vanilla**
1 tablespoon **cornstarch**

Topping:
1 cup **flour**
$^3/_4$ cup **quick oats**
1 cup **brown sugar**
2 teaspoons **cinnamon**
$^1/_2$ cup **butter** or **margarine,** melted

Place apples in Dutch oven sprayed with nonstick spray. In a saucepan, heat sugar, water, vanilla, and cornstarch until thickened. Pour evenly over apples.

In a bowl, combine topping ingredients and then sprinkle over apples. Bake at 350 degrees using 10 coals on bottom and 14 on top. Bake 60 minutes, or until apples are tender. Allow to cool 15–20 minutes before serving. Makes 12 servings.

OATMEAL COBBLER

Dutch oven size: 12-inch

1	**yellow cake mix**
1/2 cup	**butter** or **margarine**
2 cups	**quick oats**
1 can (21 ounces)	**cherry pie filling**
	vanilla ice cream

In a bowl, combine cake mix, butter, and oats until crumbly and set aside. Spoon pie filling in Dutch oven sprayed with nonstick spray. Sprinkle crumb mixture over top. Bake at 350 degrees using 10 coals on bottom and 14 on top. Bake 30 minutes, or until filling is bubbling through top. Serve warm with vanilla ice cream. Makes 12 servings.

VARIATION: Any flavor of fruit pie filling may be used.

SNACK CAKE

Dutch oven size: 14-inch

I can (29 ounces)	**pears,** with juice
4 cups	**flour**
2 cups	**sugar**
4 teaspoons	**baking soda**
I teaspoon	**salt**
4 teaspoons	**cinnamon**
I teaspoon	**nutmeg**
$^1/_2$ teaspoon	**ground cloves**
I cup	**oil**
2 cups	**brown sugar**
2 cups	**chocolate chips**

Mash pears in their juice and set aside.

In a large bowl, combine all remaining ingredients except brown sugar and chocolate chips. Add mashed pears to mixture. Pour into Dutch oven sprayed with nonstick spray. Sprinkle brown sugar and chocolate chips over top. Bake at 350 degrees using 10 coals on bottom and 18 on top. Bake 25 minutes, or until toothpick inserted in center comes out clean. Makes 16 servings.

CARAMEL APPLE COBBLER

Dutch oven size: 14-inch

4 cans (21 ounces each) **apple pie filling**
2 packages (32 ounces each) **Krusteez cinnamon crumb cake mix**
1 jar (20 ounces) **caramel ice cream topping**
vanilla ice cream

Spoon pie filling into bottom of Dutch oven. Mix cake batter according to package directions. Pour batter over pie filling. Bake at 350 degrees using 10 coals on bottom and 18 on top. Bake 30–35 minutes, or until toothpick inserted in center comes out clean. When cake is done, remove coals from bottom and place on top 3–5 minutes more to make top slightly crusty. Remove from heat. Pour caramel over top and serve with a scoop of vanilla ice cream. Makes 16 servings.

PEACHY DUMP CAKE

Dutch oven size: 12-inch

2 cans (19 ounces each)	**peaches,** drained
2	**white cake mixes**
2 cans (12 ounces each)	**lemon-lime soda**
1 package (8 ounces)	**Red Hot candies**

Place peaches evenly on bottom of Dutch oven. Sprinkle cake mix evenly over top. Pour soda over cake mix, trying to completely cover. Sprinkle Red Hots over top. Bake at 350 degrees using 10 coals on bottom and 14 on top. Bake 45–50 minutes, or until cake pulls away from sides of oven. Makes 12 servings.

NOTES

NOTES

NOTES

NOTES

NOTES

NOTES

ABOUT THE AUTHOR

Vernon Winterton has been cooking with Dutch ovens for thirty years. He is one of the founding members of the Greater Wasatch Dutch Oven Society and served two years as its assistant director.

Vernon has competed in Dutch oven cook-offs for ten years, qualifying three times to go to the world championships. He and his wife, Barbara, also enjoy entering cook-offs on a local level as well.

Married for thirty-five years, they live in Lehi City, Utah. He also has one daughter and one son, both of which have given him grandchildren he adores.